MznLnx

*Missing Links Exam Preps*

Exam Prep for

# Introduction to Economic Reasoning

## Rohlf, 7th Edition

**The MznLnx Exam Prep is your link from the texbook and lecture to your exams.**
**The MznLnx Exam Preps are unauthorized and comprehensive reviews of your textbooks.**

MznLnx

Rico
Publications

*Exam Prep for Introduction to Economic Reasoning*
7th Edition
Rohlf

*Publisher:* Raymond Houge
*Assistant Editor:* Michael Rouger
*Text and Cover Designer:* Lisa Buckner
*Marketing Manager:* Sara Swagger
*Project Manager, Editorial Production:* Jerry Emerson
*Art Director:* Vernon Lowerui

*Product Manager:* Dave Mason
*Editorial Assitant:* Rachel Guzmanji
*Pedagogy:* Debra Long
*Cover Image:* Jim Reed/Getty Images
*Text and Cover Printer:* City Printing, Inc.
*Compositor:* Media Mix, Inc.



Printed in the United States
ISBN:

For more information about our products, contact us at:
Dave.Mason@RicoPublications.com

For permission to use material from this text or product, submit a request online to:
Dave.Mason@RicoPublications.com

# Contents

# TO THE STUDENT

## COMPREHENSIVE

The *MznLnx* Exam Prep series is designed to help you pass your exams. Editors at MznLnx review your textbooks and then prepare these practice exams to help you master the textbook material. Unlike study guides, workbooks, and practice tests provided by the texbook publisher and textbook authors, *MznLnx* gives you ***all*** of the material in each chapter in exam form, not just samples, so you can be sure to nail your exam.

## MECHANICAL

The MznLnx Exam Prep series creates exams that will help you learn the subject matter as well as test you on your understanding. Each question is designed to help you master the concept. Just working through the exams, you gain an understanding of the subject--its a simple mechanical process that produces success.

## INTEGRATED STUDY GUIDE AND REVIEW

MznLnx is not just a set of exams designed to test you, its also a comprehensive review of the subject content. Each exam question is also a review of the concept, making sure that you will get the answer correct without having to go to other sources of material. You learn as you go! Its the easiest way to pass an exam.

## HUMOR

Studying can be tedious and dry. MznLnx's instructional design includes moderate humor within the exam questions on occassion, to break the tedium and revitalize the brain

1. _________s is the social science that studies the production, distribution, and consumption of goods and services. The term _________s comes from the Ancient Greek oá¼°κονομÎ¯α from oá¼¶κος (oikos, 'house') + νÏŒμος (nomos, 'custom' or 'law'), hence 'rules of the house(hold)'. Current _________ models developed out of the broader field of political economy in the late 19th century, owing to a desire to use an empirical approach more akin to the physical sciences.

a. Energy economics
b. Inflation
c. Opportunity cost
d. Economic

2. _________ is a term that refers both to:

- a formal discipline used to help appraise, or assess, the case for a project or proposal, which itself is a process known as project appraisal; and
- an informal approach to making decisions of any kind.

Under both definitions the process involves, whether explicitly or implicitly, weighing the total expected costs against the total expected benefits of one or more actions in order to choose the best or most profitable option. The formal process is often referred to as either CBA (_________) or BCost-benefit analysis

A hallmark of CBA is that all benefits and all costs are expressed in money terms, and are adjusted for the time value of money, so that all flows of benefits and flows of project costs over time (which tend to occur at different points in time) are expressed on a common basis in terms of their e;present value.e; Closely related, but slightly different, formal techniques include Cost-effectiveness analysis, Economic impact analysis, Fiscal impact analysis and Social Return on Investment(SROI) analysis. The latter builds upon the logic of _________, but differs in that it is explicitly designed to inform the practical decision-making of enterprise managers and investors focused on optimising their social and environmental impacts.

a. 130-30 fund
b. 100-year flood
c. Decision theory
d. Cost-benefit analysis

3. _________ according to Onuoha (2007) is the practice of starting new organizations or revitalizing mature organizations, particularly new businesses generally in response to identified opportunities. _________ is often a difficult undertaking, as a vast majority of new businesses fail. Entrepreneurial activities are substantially different depending on the type of organization that is being started.

a. ACCRA Cost of Living Index
b. ACEA agreement
c. Intrapreneurship
d. Entrepreneurship

4. In economics, _________ is the total supply of goods and services produced by a national economy during a specific time period. It is the total amount of goods and services in the economy available at all possible price levels.

a. Aggregation problem
b. Aggregate demand
c. Aggregate expenditure
d. Aggregate supply

5. _________ or economic opportunity loss is the value of the next best alternative foregone as the result of making a decision. _________ analysis is an important part of a company's decision-making processes but is not treated as an actual cost in any financial statement. The next best thing that a person can engage in is referred to as the _________ of doing the best thing and ignoring the next best thing to be done.

a. Opportunity cost
b. Industrial organization
c. Economic
d. Economic ideology

6. In microeconomics, _________ is quite simply the conversion of inputs into outputs. It is an economic process that uses resources to create a good or service that is suitable for exchange. This can include manufacturing, storing, shipping, and packaging.

a. Red Guards
b. MET
c. Solved
d. Production

7. In economics, the _________ can be described as we shift factors of production for making one cover service to another, the cost of producing second item increases.

a. Countercyclical
b. Heterodox economics
c. Medium of exchange
d. Law of increasing costs

8. In calculus, a function f defined on a subset of the real numbers with real values is called _________, if for all x and y such that x >≤ y one has f(x) >≤ f(y), so f preserves the order. In layman's terms, the sign of the slope is always positive (the curve tending upwards) or zero (i.e., non-decreasing, or asymptotic, or depicted as a horizontal, flat line) Likewise, a function is called monotonically decreasing (non-increasing) if, whenever x >≤ y, then f(x) >≥ f(y), so it reverses the order.

a. 130-30 fund
b. 1921 recession
c. Monotonic
d. 100-year flood

9. _________ is the increase in the amount of the goods and services produced by an economy over time. It is conventionally measured as the percent rate of increase in real gross domestic product, or real GDP. Growth is usually calculated in real terms, i.e. inflation-adjusted terms, in order to net out the effect of inflation on the price of the goods and services produced.

a. AD-IA Model
b. ACEA agreement
c. ACCRA Cost of Living Index
d. Economic growth

10. A _________ occurs when an entity spends more money than it takes in. The opposite of a _________ is a budget surplus. Debt is essentially an accumulated flow of deficits.

a. Funding body
b. Budget deficit
c. Lump-sum tax
d. Public Financial Management

11. _________ is a type of trade policy that allows traders to act and transact without interference from government. Thus, the policy permits trading partners mutual gains from trade, with goods and services produced according to the theory of comparative advantage.

Under a _________ policy, prices are a reflection of true supply and demand, and are the sole determinant of resource allocation.

a. 130-30 fund
b. 100-year flood
c. Free trade
d. 1921 recession

12. A _________ in general is a certificate of ownership that gold owners hold instead of storing the actual gold. It has both a historic meaning as a US paper currency (1882-1933) and a current meaning as a way to invest in gold. A picture of a _________ Series 1934 $100 _________, Obverse $100,000 _________, Obverse

The _________ was used from 1882 to 1933 in the United States as a form of paper currency.

a. Gold certificate
b. 130-30 fund
c. 100-year flood
d. 1921 recession

13. A _________ is an object whose consumption increases the utility of the consumer, for which the quantity demanded exceeds the quantity supplied at zero price. _________s are usually modeled as having diminishing marginal utility. The first individual purchase has high utility; the second has less.

a. Pie method
b. Good
c. Merit good
d. Composite good

14. _________ is an economic system in which wealth, and the means of producing wealth, are privately owned. Through _________, the land, labor, and capital are owned, operated, and traded for the purpose of generating profits, without force or fraud, by private individuals either singly or jointly, and investments, distribution, income, production, pricing and supply of goods, commodities and services are determined by voluntary private decision in a market economy. A distinguishing feature of _________ is that each person owns his or her own labor and therefore is allowed to sell the use of it to employers.

a. Late capitalism
b. Creative capitalism
c. Socialism for the rich and capitalism for the poor
d. Capitalism

15. _________ is an online peer-reviewed magazine published by the Agricultural ' Applied Economics Association (AAEA) for readers interested in the policy and management of agriculture, the food industry, natural resources, rural communities, and the environment. _________ is published quarterly and is available free online. It is currently one of three outreach products offered by AAEA, along with the more timely Policy Issues and the forthcoming Shared Materials section of the AAEA Web site.

a. 100-year flood
b. Choices
c. 1921 recession
d. 130-30 fund

16. _________ is used to refer to a number of related concepts. It is the using resources in such a way as to maximize the production of goods and services. A system can be called economically efficient if:

- No one can be made better off without making someone else worse off.
- More output cannot be obtained without increasing the amount of inputs.
- Production proceeds at the lowest possible per-unit cost.

These definitions of efficiency are not equivalent, but they are all encompassed by the idea that nothing more can be achieved given the resources available.

An economic system is more efficient if it can provide more goods and services for society without using more resources.

a. ACEA agreement
b. Economic efficiency
c. Efficient contract theory
d. ACCRA Cost of Living Index

17. _________ is one of the four Ps of the marketing mix. The other three aspects are product, promotion, and place. It is also a key variable in microeconomic price allocation theory.

a. Premium pricing
b. Point of total assumption
c. Guaranteed Maximum Price
d. Pricing

18. _________ in economics and business is the result of an exchange and from that trade we assign a numerical monetary value to a good, service or asset. If Alice trades Bob 4 apples for an orange, the _________ of an orange is 4 apples. Inversely, the _________ of an apple is 1/4 oranges.

a. Price war
b. Premium pricing
c. Price book
d. Price

19. In economics, _________ is the total demand for final goods and services in the economy (Y) at a given time and price level. It is the amount of goods and services in the economy that will be purchased at all possible price levels. This is the demand for the gross domestic product of a country when inventory levels are static.

a. Aggregate supply
b. Aggregate demand
c. Aggregation problem
d. Aggregate expenditure

20. Economics:

- _________,the desire to own something and the ability to pay for it
- _________ curve,a graphic representation of a _________ schedule
- _________ deposit, the money in checking accounts
- _________ pull theory,the theory that inflation occurs when _________ for goods and services exceeds existing supplies
- _________ schedule,a table that lists the quantity of a good a person will buy it each different price
- _________ side economics,the school of economics at believes government spending and tax cuts open economy by raising _________

.

a. Variability
b. Production
c. Demand
d. McKesson ' Robbins scandal

21. _________ in political thought refers to economic theories of social organization advocating collective ownership and administration of the means of production and distribution of goods, and a society characterized by equality for all individuals, with an egalitarian method of compensation. Modern _________ originated in the late 19th-century intellectual and working class political movement that criticized the effects of industrialization and private ownership on society. Karl Marx posited that _________ would be achieved via class struggle and a proletarian revolution after a transitional stage from capitalism called the dictatorship of the proletariat.

a. Adolph Fischer
b. Socialism
c. Adam Smith
d. Adolf Hitler

22. In macroeconomics, _________ is a condition of the national economy, where all or nearly all persons willing and able to work at the prevailing wages and working conditions are able to do so. It is defined either as 0% unemployment, literally, no unemployment (the rate of unemployment is the fraction of the work force unable to find work), as by James Tobin, or as the level of employment rates when there is no cyclical unemployment. It is defined by the majority of mainstream economists as being an acceptable level of natural unemployment above 0%, the discrepancy from 0% being due to non-cyclical types of unemployment.

a. Demand shock
b. Harrod-Johnson diagram
c. Full employment
d. Marginal propensity to consume

23. _________ is a practice of protecting the environment, on individual, organisational or governmental level, for the benefit of the natural environment and (or) humans.

Due to the pressures of population and technology the biophysical environment is being degraded, sometimes permanently. This has been recognised and governments began placing restraints on activities that caused environmental degradation.

a. AD-IA Model
b. ACEA agreement
c. ACCRA Cost of Living Index
d. Environmental protection

24. _________ is a common concept in economics, and gives rise to derived concepts such as consumer debt. Generally _________ is defined by opposition to production. But the precise definition can vary because different schools of economists define production quite differently.

a. Cash or share options
b. Foreclosure data providers
c. Federal Reserve Bank Notes
d. Consumption

25. CÄ"terÄ«s paribus is a Latin phrase, literally translated as 'with other things the same.' It is commonly rendered in English as 'all other things being equal.' A prediction, or a statement about causal or logical connections between two states of affairs, is qualified by _________ in order to acknowledge, and to rule out, the possibility of other factors which could override the relationship between the antecedent and the consequent.

A _________ assumption is often fundamental to the predictive purpose of scientific inquiry. In order to formulate scientific laws, it is usually necessary to rule out factors which interfere with examining a specific causal relationship.

a. Dematerialization
b. Ceteris paribus
c. Friedman-Savage utility function
d. Capital outflow

26. _________ is a branch of economics with three main subdisciplines international trade, monetary economics and international finance.

- International trade studies goods-and-services flows across international boundaries from supply-and-demand factors, economic integration, and policy variables such as tariff rates and trade quotas.
- International finance studies the flow of capital across international financial markets, and the effects of these movements on exchange rates.
- International monetary economics and macroeconomics studies money and macro flows across countries.

- Stanley W. Black (2008.) 'international monetary institutions,' The New Palgrave Dictionary of Economics. 2nd Edition.

a. ACCRA Cost of Living Index
b. Index number
c. International economics
d. Economic depreciation

27. _________ is a branch of economics that deals with the performance, structure, and behavior of a national or regional economy as a whole. Along with microeconomics, _________ is one of the two most general fields in economics. It is the study of the behavior and decision-making of entire economies.

a. New Trade Theory
b. Macroeconomics
c. Tobit model
d. Nominal value

28. _________ is a branch of economics that studies how individuals, households and firms and some states make decisions to allocate limited resources, typically in markets where goods or services are being bought and sold. _________ examines how these decisions and behaviours affect the supply and demand for goods and services, which determines prices; and how prices, in turn , determine the supply and demand of goods and services.

Whereas macroeconomics involves the 'sum total of economic activity, dealing with the issues of growth, inflation and unemployment, and with national economic policies relating to these issues' and the effects of government actions on them.

a. New Keynesian economics
b. Countercyclical
c. Recession
d. Microeconomics

1. _________s is the social science that studies the production, distribution, and consumption of goods and services. The term _________s comes from the Ancient Greek oá¼°κονομÎ¯α from oá¼¶κος (oikos, 'house') + νÏŒμος (nomos, 'custom' or 'law'), hence 'rules of the house(hold)'. Current _________ models developed out of the broader field of political economy in the late 19th century, owing to a desire to use an empirical approach more akin to the physical sciences.

a. Energy economics
b. Inflation
c. Opportunity cost
d. Economic

2. An _________ or Å"conomic system is a system that involves the production, distribution and consumption of goods and services between the entities in a particular society. It is the method used by society to produce and distribute goods and services. The _________ is composed of people and institutions, including their relationships to productive resources, such as through the convention of property.

a. Indicative planning
b. Intention economy
c. Information economy
d. Economic system

3. _________ is an economic system in which wealth, and the means of producing wealth, are privately owned. Through _________, the land, labor, and capital are owned, operated, and traded for the purpose of generating profits, without force or fraud, by private individuals either singly or jointly, and investments, distribution, income, production, pricing and supply of goods, commodities and services are determined by voluntary private decision in a market economy. A distinguishing feature of _________ is that each person owns his or her own labor and therefore is allowed to sell the use of it to employers.

a. Creative capitalism
b. Late capitalism
c. Socialism for the rich and capitalism for the poor
d. Capitalism

4. In statistics, _________ has two related meanings:

- the arithmetic _________
- the expected value of a random variable, which is also called the population _________.

It is sometimes stated that the '_________' _________s average. This is incorrect if '_________' is taken in the specific sense of 'arithmetic _________' as there are different types of averages: the _________, median, and mode. Other simple statistical analyses use measures of spread, such as range, interquartile range, or standard deviation. For a real-valued random variable X, the _________ is the expectation of X. Note that not every probability distribution has a defined _________ (or variance); see the Cauchy distribution for an example.

a. Mean
b. 130-30 fund
c. 1921 recession
d. 100-year flood

5. In microeconomics, _________ is quite simply the conversion of inputs into outputs. It is an economic process that uses resources to create a good or service that is suitable for exchange. This can include manufacturing, storing, shipping, and packaging.

a. Production
b. Solved
c. MET
d. Red Guards

6. In economics, the term _________ of income or _________ refers to a simple economic model which describes the reciprocal circulation of income between producers and consumers. In the _________ model, the inter-dependent entities of producer and consumer are referred to as 'firms' and 'households' respectively and provide each other with factors in order to facilitate the flow of income. Firms provide consumers with goods and services in exchange for consumer expenditure and 'factors of production' from households.

a. 100-year flood
b. 1921 recession
c. 130-30 fund
d. Circular flow

7. _________ was a survey conducted by the U.S. Department of Justice to gauge the prevalence of alcohol and illegal drug use among prior arrestees. It was a reformulation of the prior Drug Use Forecasting (DUF) program, focused on five drugs in particular: cocaine, marijuana, methamphetamine, opiates, and PCP.

Participants were randomly selected from arrest records in major metropolitan areas; because no personally identifying information is taken from each record chosen, the resulting data can be correlated to arrest rates, but not to the total population of persons charged.

a. AD-IA Model
b. ACCRA Cost of Living Index
c. ACEA agreement
d. Arrestee Drug Abuse Monitoring

8. In economics, the _________ is the term economists use to describe the self-regulating nature of the marketplace. The _________ is a metaphor coined by the economist Adam Smith in The Wealth of Nations.

Adam Smith mentions the metaphor in Book IV of The Wealth of Nations, arguing that people in any society will certainly employ their capital in foreign trading only if the profits available by that method far exceed those available locally, and that in such a case it is better for society as a whole if they so did.

a. ACCRA Cost of Living Index
b. Invisible hand
c. ACEA agreement
d. AD-IA Model

9. _________ is an economic concept with commonplace familiarity. It is the price that a good or service is offered at, or will fetch, in the marketplace. It is of interest mainly in the study of microeconomics.

a. Paper trading
b. Noisy market hypothesis
c. Market price
d. Market anomaly

10. _________ was a Scottish moral philosopher and a pioneer of political economy. One of the key figures of the Scottish Enlightenment, Smith is the author of The Theory of Moral Sentiments and An Inquiry into the Nature and Causes of the Wealth of Nations. The latter, usually abbreviated as The Wealth of Nations, is considered his magnum opus and the first modern work of economics.

a. Alan Greenspan
b. Adolph Fischer
c. Adolf Hitler
d. Adam Smith

11. _________ in economics and business is the result of an exchange and from that trade we assign a numerical monetary value to a good, service or asset. If Alice trades Bob 4 apples for an orange, the _________ of an orange is 4 apples. Inversely, the _________ of an apple is 1/4 oranges.

a. Price war
b. Price book
c. Premium pricing
d. Price

12. The _________ is 'the basic residential unit in which economic production, consumption, inheritance, child rearing, and shelter are organized and carried out'; [the _________] 'may or may not be synonomous with family'.

The _________ is the basic unit of analysis in many social, microeconomic and government models. The term refers to all individuals who live in the same dwelling.

a. Household
b. Family economics
c. 130-30 fund
d. 100-year flood

13. _________ is a term used to describe a policy of allowing events to take their own course. The term is a French phrase literally meaning 'let do'. It is a doctrine that states that government generally should not intervene in the marketplace.

a. Laissez-faire
b. Communization
c. Theory of Productive Forces
d. Heroic capitalism

14. In economics, the _________ is a subset of the domestic economy excluding the economic activities of general government, private households, and nonprofit organizations serving individuals. In the United States the _________ accounted for about 78 percent of the value of gross domestic product (GDP) in 2000. .

a. Reaganomics
b. Happiness economics
c. Social savings
d. Business sector

15. _________ is a mechanism that allows people easily to buy and sell products. Services are often included in the scope of the term. _________ regulation is an economic term that describes restrictions in the market.

a. Fixed exchange rate system
b. Product market
c. Market dominance
d. Financialization

16. _________ is a broad label that refers to any individuals or households that use goods and services generated within the economy. The concept of a _________ is used in different contexts, so that the usage and significance of the term may vary.

Typically when business people and economists talk of _________s they are talking about person as _________, an aggregated commodity item with little individuality other than that expressed in the buy/not-buy decision.

a. 130-30 fund
b. 100-year flood
c. 1921 recession
d. Consumer

17. _________ is a term which is used in economics to refer to the rule or sovereignty of purchasers in markets as to production of goods. It is the power of consumers to decide what gets produced. People use the this term to describe the consumer as the 'king,' or ruler, of the market, the one who determines what products will be produced.

a. Microeconomic reform
b. Consumer sovereignty
c. Schedule delay
d. Reservation price

18. _________ is used to refer to a number of related concepts. It is the using resources in such a way as to maximize the production of goods and services. A system can be called economically efficient if:

- No one can be made better off without making someone else worse off.
- More output cannot be obtained without increasing the amount of inputs.
- Production proceeds at the lowest possible per-unit cost.

These definitions of efficiency are not equivalent, but they are all encompassed by the idea that nothing more can be achieved given the resources available.

An economic system is more efficient if it can provide more goods and services for society without using more resources.

a. ACCRA Cost of Living Index
b. Efficient contract theory
c. Economic efficiency
d. ACEA agreement

19. _________ was an American economist, statistician and public intellectual, and a recipient of the Nobel Memorial Prize in Economic Sciences. He is best known among scholars for his theoretical and empirical research, especially consumption analysis, monetary history and theory, and for his demonstration of the complexity of stabilization policy. A global public followed his restatement of a political philosophy that insisted on minimizing the role of government in favor of the private sector.

a. Adolph Fischer
b. Adam Smith
c. Adolf Hitler
d. Milton Friedman

20. _________ is a practice of protecting the environment, on individual, organisational or governmental level, for the benefit of the natural environment and (or) humans.

Due to the pressures of population and technology the biophysical environment is being degraded, sometimes permanently. This has been recognised and governments began placing restraints on activities that caused environmental degradation.

a. AD-IA Model
b. ACEA agreement
c. ACCRA Cost of Living Index
d. Environmental protection

21. _________ in political thought refers to economic theories of social organization advocating collective ownership and administration of the means of production and distribution of goods, and a society characterized by equality for all individuals, with an egalitarian method of compensation. Modern _________ originated in the late 19th-century intellectual and working class political movement that criticized the effects of industrialization and private ownership on society. Karl Marx posited that _________ would be achieved via class struggle and a proletarian revolution after a transitional stage from capitalism called the dictatorship of the proletariat.

a. Adolf Hitler
b. Adolph Fischer
c. Adam Smith
d. Socialism

22. Economic interventionism or _________ is an action in a Market economy taken by a government, beyond the basic regulation of fraud and enforcement of contracts, in an effort to affect its own economy. Economic intervention can be aimed at a variety of political or economic objectives, such as promoting economic growth, increasing employment, raising wages, raising or reducing prices, promoting equality, managing the money supply and interest rates, increasing profits, or addressing market failures. The intervention may to direct, or indirect as in the case of indicative planning.

a. ACCRA Cost of Living Index
b. ACEA agreement
c. AD-IA Model
d. Economic planning

23. _________ is used to assign the available resources in an economic way. It is part of resource management.

In strategic planning,is a plan for using available resources, for example human resources, especially in the near term, to achieve goals for the future.

a. 1921 recession
b. 130-30 fund
c. 100-year flood
d. Resource allocation

24. In economics, an externality or spillover of an economic transaction is an impact on a party that is not directly involved in the transaction. In such a case, prices do not reflect the full costs or benefits in production or consumption of a product or service. A positive impact is called an _________, while a negative impact is called an external cost.

a. ACEA agreement
b. AD-IA Model
c. ACCRA Cost of Living Index
d. External benefit

25. _________ is the increase in the amount of the goods and services produced by an economy over time. It is conventionally measured as the percent rate of increase in real gross domestic product, or real GDP. Growth is usually calculated in real terms, i.e. inflation-adjusted terms, in order to net out the effect of inflation on the price of the goods and services produced.

a. Economic growth
b. ACCRA Cost of Living Index
c. AD-IA Model
d. ACEA agreement

26. A _________ occurs when an entity spends more money than it takes in. The opposite of a _________ is a budget surplus. Debt is essentially an accumulated flow of deficits.

a. Budget deficit
b. Funding body
c. Public Financial Management
d. Lump-sum tax

27. Many _________ are related to the environmental consequences of production and use

- Systemic risk describes the risks to the overall economy arising from the risks which the banking system takes. That the private costs of banking failure may be smaller than the social costs justifies banking regulations, although regulations could create a moral hazard.

- Anthropogenic climate change is attributed to greenhouse gas emissions from burning oil, gas, and coal. Global warming has been ranked as the #1 externality of all economic activity, in the magnitude of potential harms and yet remains unmitigated.

a. Total Economic Value
b. Negative externalities
c. Green certificate
d. White certificates

28. A _________ in general is a certificate of ownership that gold owners hold instead of storing the actual gold. It has both a historic meaning as a US paper currency (1882-1933) and a current meaning as a way to invest in gold. A picture of a _________ Series 1934 $100 _________, Obverse $100,000 _________, Obverse

The _________ was used from 1882 to 1933 in the United States as a form of paper currency.

a. 100-year flood
b. 130-30 fund
c. 1921 recession
d. Gold certificate

29. A _________ is an object whose consumption increases the utility of the consumer, for which the quantity demanded exceeds the quantity supplied at zero price. _________s are usually modeled as having diminishing marginal utility. The first individual purchase has high utility; the second has less.

a. Pie method
b. Composite good
c. Merit good
d. Good

30. An _________ is a tax levied on the financial income of people, corporations, or other legal entities. Various _________ systems exist, with varying degrees of tax incidence. Income taxation can be progressive, proportional, or regressive.

a. AD-IA Model
b. ACCRA Cost of Living Index
c. Income tax
d. ACEA agreement

31. In economics, a _________ is a good that is non-rivaled and non-excludable. This means, respectively, that consumption of the good by one individual does not reduce availability of the good for consumption by others; and that no one can be effectively excluded from using the good. In the real world, there may be no such thing as an absolutely non-rivaled and non-excludable good; but economists think that some goods approximate the concept closely enough for the analysis to be economically useful.

a. Neoclassical synthesis
b. Public good
c. Demand-pull theory
d. Happiness economics

32. To _________ is to impose a financial charge or other levy upon a taxpayer by a state or the functional equivalent of a state.

_________es are also imposed by many subnational entities. _________es consist of direct _________ or indirect _________, and may be paid in money or as its labour equivalent (often but not always unpaid.)

a. 130-30 fund
b. 1921 recession
c. 100-year flood
d. Tax

33. To tax is to impose a financial charge or other levy upon a taxpayer by a state or the functional equivalent of a state.

_________ are also imposed by many subnational entities. _________ consist of direct tax or indirect tax, and may be paid in money or as its labour equivalent (often but not always unpaid.)

a. 1921 recession
b. 130-30 fund
c. 100-year flood
d. Taxes

34. _________ is an online peer-reviewed magazine published by the Agricultural ' Applied Economics Association (AAEA) for readers interested in the policy and management of agriculture, the food industry, natural resources, rural communities, and the environment. _________ is published quarterly and is available free online. It is currently one of three outreach products offered by AAEA, along with the more timely Policy Issues and the forthcoming Shared Materials section of the AAEA Web site.

a. 100-year flood
b. 130-30 fund
c. 1921 recession
d. Choices

35. In mathematics, an _________ is a statement about the relative size or order of two objects, or about whether they are the same or not

- The notation a < b means that a is less than b.
- The notation a > b means that a is greater than b.
- The notation a ≠ b means that a is not equal to b, but does not say that one is greater than the other or even that they can be compared in size.

In each statement above, a is not equal to b. These relations are known as strict inequalities. The notation a < b may also be read as 'a is strictly less than b'.

a. AD-IA Model
b. ACCRA Cost of Living Index
c. ACEA agreement
d. Inequality

36. Discounting is a financial mechanism in which a debtor obtains the right to delay payments to a creditor, for a defined period of time, in exchange for a charge or fee. Essentially, the party that owes money in the present purchases the right to delay the payment until some future date. The _________, or charge, is simply the difference between the original amount owed in the present and the amount that has to be paid in the future to settle the debt.

a. Reinsurance
b. Reliability theory
c. Certified Risk Manager
d. Discount

37. The _________ is an interest rate a central bank charges depository institutions that borrow reserves from it.

The term _________ has two meanings:

- the same as interest rate; the term 'discount' does not refer to the meaning of the word, but to the purpose of using the quantity, such as computations of present value, e.g. net present value or discounted cash flow

- the annual effective _________, which is the annual interest divided by the capital including that interest; this rate is lower than the interest rate; it corresponds to using the value after a year as the nominal value, and seeing the initial value as the nominal value minus a discount; it is used for Treasury Bills and similar financial instruments

The annual effective _________ is the annual interest divided by the capital including that interest, which is the interest rate divided by 100% plus the interest rate. It is the annual discount factor to be applied to the future cash flow, to find the discount, subtracted from a future value to find the value one year earlier.

For example, suppose there is a government bond that sells for $95 and pays $100 in a year's time.

a. Perpetuity
b. Johansen test
c. Stochastic volatility
d. Discount rate

38. A _________ is an economic system that incorporates a mixture of private and government ownership or control, or a mixture of capitalism and socialism.

There is not one single definition for a _________, but relevant aspects include: a degree of private economic freedom (including privately owned industry) intermingled with centralized economic planning and government regulation (which may include regulation of the market for environmental concerns and social welfare, or state ownership and management of some of the means of production for national or social objectives.)

For some states, there is not a consensus on whether they are capitalist, socialist, or mixed economies.

a. Mixed economy
b. Planned liberalism
c. Hunter-gatherer
d. Dual economy

39.

_________ was the last General Secretary of the Communist Party of the Soviet Union, serving from 1985 until 1991, and also the last head of state of the USSR, serving from 1988 until its collapse in 1991. He was the only Soviet leader to have been born after the October Revolution of 1917.

Gorbachev was born in Stavropol Krai into a peasant family, and operated combine harvesters on collective farms.

a. Adam Smith
b. Adolph Fischer
c. Mikhail Sergeyevich Gorbachev
d. Adolf Hitler

40. The post-Soviet states, also commonly known as the _________ or former Soviet republics, are the 15 independent nations that split off from the Union of Soviet Socialist Republics in its breakup in December 1991. Excluding the Baltic states (which were independent before World War II and already in 1989 signalled their political intention to dissociate themselves from the rest of the Soviet Union), they were also referred to as the Newly Independent States (NIS.) Post-Soviet states in English alphabetical order:1.

a. 1921 recession
b. Former Soviet Union
c. 100-year flood
d. 130-30 fund

41. _________ was a prominent Chinese politician. As leader of the Communist Party of China, Deng became a reformer who led China towards market economics. While Deng never held office as the head of state or the head of government, he nonetheless served as the Paramount leader of the People's Republic of China from 1978 to the early 1990s.

a. Adolf Hitler
b. Adam Smith
c. Adolph Fischer
d. Deng Xiaoping

42. _________ was an American industrialist and philanthropist. Rockefeller revolutionized the petroleum industry and defined the structure of modern philanthropy. In 1870, he founded the Standard Oil Company and ran it until he officially retired in 1897.

a. Adam Smith
b. Adolf Hitler
c. Adolph Fischer
d. John Davison Rockefeller

43. A _________ is an agreement between businesses, usually motivated by cost reduction and improved service for the customer. Alliances are often bounded by a single agreement with equitable risk and opportunity share for all parties involved and are typically managed by an integrated project team. An example of this is code sharing in airline alliances.

a. Market entry
b. Golden parachute
c. Business alliance
d. Golden Boot Compensation

1. _________ in economics and business is the result of an exchange and from that trade we assign a numerical monetary value to a good, service or asset. If Alice trades Bob 4 apples for an orange, the _________ of an orange is 4 apples. Inversely, the _________ of an apple is 1/4 oranges.

a. Price book
b. Price war
c. Premium pricing
d. Price

2. In economics, _________ is the total demand for final goods and services in the economy (Y) at a given time and price level. It is the amount of goods and services in the economy that will be purchased at all possible price levels. This is the demand for the gross domestic product of a country when inventory levels are static.

a. Aggregation problem
b. Aggregate supply
c. Aggregate expenditure
d. Aggregate demand

3. Economics:

- _________,the desire to own something and the ability to pay for it
- _________ curve,a graphic representation of a _________ schedule
- _________ deposit, the money in checking accounts
- _________ pull theory,the theory that inflation occurs when _________ for goods and services exceeds existing supplies
- _________ schedule,a table that lists the quantity of a good a person will buy it each different price
- _________ side economics,the school of economics at believes government spending and tax cuts open economy by raising _________

.

a. Demand
b. McKesson ' Robbins scandal
c. Production
d. Variability

4. In economics, _________ is the ratio of the percent change in one variable to the percent change in another variable. It is a tool for measuring the responsiveness of a function to changes in parameters in a relative way. Commonly analyzed are _________ of substitution, price and wealth.

a. ACEA agreement
b. Elasticity of demand
c. ACCRA Cost of Living Index
d. Elasticity

5. Price _________ is defined as the measure of responsiveness in the quantity demanded for a commodity as a result of change in price of the same commodity. It is a measure of how consumers react to a change in price. In other words, it is percentage change in quantity demanded by the percentage change in price of the same commodity.

a. ACEA agreement
b. Elasticity of demand
c. Elasticity
d. ACCRA Cost of Living Index

6. In economics, the _________ can be defined as the graph depicting the relationship between the price of a certain commodity, and the amount of it that consumers are willing and able to purchase at that given price. It is a graphic representation of a demand schedule. The _________ for all consumers together follows from the _________ of every individual consumer: the individual demands at each price are added together.

a. Cost curve
b. Demand curve
c. Wage curve
d. Kuznets curve

7. In algebra, a _________ is a function depending on n that associates a scalar, det(A), to an n×n square matrix A. The fundamental geometric meaning of a _________ is a scale factor for measure when A is regarded as a linear transformation. _________s are important both in calculus, where they enter the substitution rule for several variables, and in multilinear algebra.

For a fixed nonnegative integer n, there is a unique _________ function for the n×n matrices over any commutative ring R. In particular, this function exists when R is the field of real or complex numbers.

a. Determinant
b. 130-30 fund
c. 100-year flood
d. 1921 recession

8. In economics, the _________ is the change in consumption resulting from a change in real income.

Another important item that can change is the money income of the consumer. The _________ is the phenomenon observed through changes in purchasing power.

a. Export subsidy
b. Inflation hedge
c. Equilibrium wage
d. Income effect

9. In economics, the _________ is an economic law that states that consumers buy more of a good when its price decreases and less when its price increases.

There are certain goods which do not follow this law. These include Veblen and Giffen goods

a. Georgism
b. Financial crisis
c. Market failure
d. Law of demand

10. A _________ in general is a certificate of ownership that gold owners hold instead of storing the actual gold. It has both a historic meaning as a US paper currency (1882-1933) and a current meaning as a way to invest in gold. A picture of a _________ Series 1934 $100 _________, Obverse $100,000 _________, Obverse

The _________ was used from 1882 to 1933 in the United States as a form of paper currency.

a. 100-year flood
b. Gold certificate
c. 130-30 fund
d. 1921 recession

11. A _________ is an object whose consumption increases the utility of the consumer, for which the quantity demanded exceeds the quantity supplied at zero price. _________s are usually modeled as having diminishing marginal utility. The first individual purchase has high utility; the second has less.

a. Merit good
b. Good
c. Pie method
d. Composite good

12. In consumer theory, an _________ is a good that decreases in demand when consumer income rises, unlike normal goods, for which the opposite is observed. It is a good that consumers demand increases when their income increases. Inferiority, in this sense, is an observable fact relating to affordability rather than a statement about the quality of the good.

a. Export-oriented
b. Independent goods
c. Information good
d. Inferior good

13. In economics, _________s are any goods for which demand increases when income increases and falls when income decreases but price remains constant, i.e. with a positive income elasticity of demand. The term does not necessarily refer to the quality of the good.

Depending on the indifference curves, the amount of a good bought can either increase, decrease, or stay the same when income increases.

a. Bord halfpenny
b. Financial contagion
c. Normative economics
d. Normal good

14. _________ is an online peer-reviewed magazine published by the Agricultural ' Applied Economics Association (AAEA) for readers interested in the policy and management of agriculture, the food industry, natural resources, rural communities, and the environment. _________ is published quarterly and is available free online. It is currently one of three outreach products offered by AAEA, along with the more timely Policy Issues and the forthcoming Shared Materials section of the AAEA Web site.

a. 1921 recession
b. 130-30 fund
c. 100-year flood
d. Choices

15. _________ is a broad label that refers to any individuals or households that use goods and services generated within the economy. The concept of a _________ is used in different contexts, so that the usage and significance of the term may vary.

Typically when business people and economists talk of _________s they are talking about person as _________, an aggregated commodity item with little individuality other than that expressed in the buy/not-buy decision.

a. 1921 recession
b. 100-year flood
c. 130-30 fund
d. Consumer

16. In economics, the _________ is defined as a numerical measure of the responsiveness of the quantity supplied of product (A) to a change in price of product (A) alone. It is the measure of the way quantity supplied reacts to a change in price.

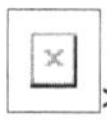

>

For example, if, in response to a 10% rise in the price of a good, the quantity supplied increases by 20%, the _________ would be 20%/10% = 2.

a. Demand shaping
b. Hedonimetry
c. Passive income
d. Price elasticity of supply

17. In economics, the _________ is the tendency of suppliers to offer more of a good at a higher price. The relationship between price and quantity supplied is usually a positive relationship. A rise in price is associated with a rise in quantity supplied.

a. Mathematical economics
b. Heterodox economics
c. Law of supply
d. Market failure

18. Competition law, known in the United States as _________ law, has three main elements:

- prohibiting agreements or practices that restrict free trading and competition between business entities. This includes in particular the repression of cartels.
- banning abusive behaviour by a firm dominating a market, or anti-competitive practices that tend to lead to such a dominant position. Practices controlled in this way may include predatory pricing, tying, price gouging, refusal to deal, and many others.
- supervising the mergers and acquisitions of large corporations, including some joint ventures. Transactions that are considered to threaten the competitive process can be prohibited altogether, or approved subject to 'remedies' such as an obligation to divest part of the merged business or to offer licences or access to facilities to enable other businesses to continue competing.

The substance and practice of competition law varies from jurisdiction to jurisdiction. Protecting the interests of consumers (consumer welfare) and ensuring that entrepreneurs have an opportunity to compete in the market economy are often treated as important objectives. Competition law is closely connected with law on deregulation of access to markets, state aids and subsidies, the privatisation of state owned assets and the establishment of independent sector regulators. In recent decades, competition law has been viewed as a way to provide better public services.

a. Antitrust
b. Anti-Inflation Act
c. United Kingdom competition law
d. Intellectual property law

19. In economics, _________ is the total supply of goods and services produced by a national economy during a specific time period. It is the total amount of goods and services in the economy available at all possible price levels.

a. Aggregation problem
b. Aggregate expenditure
c. Aggregate demand
d. Aggregate supply

20. _________ is the controlled distribution of resources and scarce goods or services. _________ controls the size of the ration, one's allotted portion of the resources being distributed on a particular day or at a particular time.

In economics, it is often common to use the word '_________' to refer to one of the roles that prices play in markets, while _________ is called 'non-price _________.' Using prices to ration means that those with the most money (or other assets) and who want a product the most are first to receive it.

a. 1921 recession
b. 130-30 fund
c. Rationing
d. 100-year flood

21. _________s is the social science that studies the production, distribution, and consumption of goods and services. The term _________s comes from the Ancient Greek oá¼°κονομÍ¯α from oá¼¶κος (oikos, 'house') + νÏŒμος (nomos, 'custom' or 'law'), hence 'rules of the house(hold)'. Current _________ models developed out of the broader field of political economy in the late 19th century, owing to a desire to use an empirical approach more akin to the physical sciences.

a. Energy economics
b. Economic
c. Inflation
d. Opportunity cost

22. _________ is used to refer to a number of related concepts. It is the using resources in such a way as to maximize the production of goods and services. A system can be called economically efficient if:

- No one can be made better off without making someone else worse off.
- More output cannot be obtained without increasing the amount of inputs.
- Production proceeds at the lowest possible per-unit cost.

These definitions of efficiency are not equivalent, but they are all encompassed by the idea that nothing more can be achieved given the resources available.

An economic system is more efficient if it can provide more goods and services for society without using more resources.

a. ACCRA Cost of Living Index
b. ACEA agreement
c. Economic efficiency
d. Efficient contract theory

23. _________ is an economic system in which wealth, and the means of producing wealth, are privately owned. Through _________, the land, labor, and capital are owned, operated, and traded for the purpose of generating profits, without force or fraud, by private individuals either singly or jointly, and investments, distribution, income, production, pricing and supply of goods, commodities and services are determined by voluntary private decision in a market economy. A distinguishing feature of _________ is that each person owns his or her own labor and therefore is allowed to sell the use of it to employers.

a. Socialism for the rich and capitalism for the poor
b. Creative capitalism
c. Late capitalism
d. Capitalism

1. _________s is the social science that studies the production, distribution, and consumption of goods and services. The term _________s comes from the Ancient Greek οá¼°κονομÎ¯α from οá¼¶κος (oikos, 'house') + νÏŒμος (nomos, 'custom' or 'law'), hence 'rules of the house(hold)'. Current _________ models developed out of the broader field of political economy in the late 19th century, owing to a desire to use an empirical approach more akin to the physical sciences.

a. Inflation
b. Opportunity cost
c. Energy economics
d. Economic

2. The term _________ refers to government debt, expenditures and revenues, or to finance (particularly financial revenue) in general.

- _________ deficit is the budget deficit of federal or local government
- _________ policy is the discretionary spending of governments. Contrasts with monetary policy.
- _________ year and _________ quarter are reporting periods for firms and other agencies.

.

a. Procter ' Gamble
b. Fiscal
c. Bucket shop
d. Drawdown

3. In economics, _________ is the use of government spending and revenue collection to influence the economy.

_________ can be contrasted with the other main type of economic policy, monetary policy, which attempts to stabilize the economy by controlling interest rates and the supply of money. The two main instruments of _________ are government spending and taxation.

a. 100-year flood
b. Fiscalism
c. Fiscal policy
d. Sustainable investment rule

4. _________ is the process by which the government, central bank (ii) availability of money, and (iii) cost of money or rate of interest, in order to attain a set of objectives oriented towards the growth and stability of the economy. Monetary theory provides insight into how to craft optimal _________.

_________ is referred to as either being an expansionary policy where an expansionary policy increases the total supply of money in the economy, and a contractionary policy decreases the total money supply.

a. 1921 recession
b. 130-30 fund
c. 100-year flood
d. Monetary policy

5. _________ in economics and business is the result of an exchange and from that trade we assign a numerical monetary value to a good, service or asset. If Alice trades Bob 4 apples for an orange, the _________ of an orange is 4 apples. Inversely, the _________ of an apple is 1/4 oranges.

a. Premium pricing
b. Price
c. Price book
d. Price war

6. In economics, a _________ may be either a subsidy or a price control, both with the intended effect of keeping the market price of a good higher than the competitive equilibrium level.

In the case of a price control, a _________ is the minimum legal price a seller may charge, typically placed above equilibrium. It is the support of certain price levels at or above market values by the government.

a. Payment schedule
b. Labor intensity
c. Price support
d. Marginal profit

7. To _________ is to impose a financial charge or other levy upon a taxpayer by a state or the functional equivalent of a state.

_________es are also imposed by many subnational entities. _________es consist of direct _________ or indirect _________, and may be paid in money or as its labour equivalent (often but not always unpaid.)

a. 130-30 fund
b. 1921 recession
c. Tax
d. 100-year flood

8. In economics, _________ is the total demand for final goods and services in the economy (Y) at a given time and price level. It is the amount of goods and services in the economy that will be purchased at all possible price levels. This is the demand for the gross domestic product of a country when inventory levels are static.
a. Aggregate expenditure
b. Aggregate demand
c. Aggregation problem
d. Aggregate supply

9. Economics:

- _________,the desire to own something and the ability to pay for it
- _________ curve,a graphic representation of a _________ schedule
- _________ deposit, the money in checking accounts
- _________ pull theory,the theory that inflation occurs when _________ for goods and services exceeds existing supplies
- _________ schedule,a table that lists the quantity of a good a person will buy it each different price
- _________ side economics,the school of economics at believes government spending and tax cuts open economy by raising _________

.

a. Production
b. McKesson ' Robbins scandal
c. Demand
d. Variability

10. _________ is one of the four Ps of the marketing mix. The other three aspects are product, promotion, and place. It is also a key variable in microeconomic price allocation theory.
a. Premium pricing
b. Guaranteed Maximum Price
c. Point of total assumption
d. Pricing

11. A _________ is the lowest hourly, daily or monthly wage that employers may legally pay to employees or workers. Equivalently, it is the lowest wage at which workers may sell their labor. Although _________ laws are in effect in a great many jurisdictions, there are differences of opinion about the benefits and drawbacks of a _________.

a. Permanent war economy
b. Marginal propensity to consume
c. Microfoundations
d. Minimum wage

12. A _________ is a government imposed limit on how high a price can be charged on a product. For a _________ to be effective, it must differ from the free market price. In the graph at right, the supply and demand curves intersect to determine the free-market quantity and price.

a. Fire sale
b. Pricing
c. Product sabotage
d. Price ceiling

13. Economic _________ is defined as an excess distribution to any factor in a production process above that which is required to induce the factor into the process or any excess above that which is necessary to keep the factor in its current use..

Classical Factor _________ is primarily concerned with the fee paid for the use of fixed (e.g. natural) resources. The classical definition is expressed as any excess payment above that required to induce or provide for production.

a. 100-year flood
b. 1921 recession
c. Rent
d. 130-30 fund

14. _________ is the controlled distribution of resources and scarce goods or services. _________ controls the size of the ration, one's allotted portion of the resources being distributed on a particular day or at a particular time.

In economics, it is often common to use the word '_________' to refer to one of the roles that prices play in markets, while _________ is called 'non-price _________.' Using prices to ration means that those with the most money (or other assets) and who want a product the most are first to receive it.

a. 100-year flood
b. 130-30 fund
c. 1921 recession
d. Rationing

15. _________ refers to laws or ordinances that set price controls on the renting of residential housing. It functions as a price ceiling.

_________ exists in approximately 40 countries around the world.

a. Rent control
b. Tenant rights
c. National Housing Conference
d. 100-year flood

16. To tax is to impose a financial charge or other levy upon a taxpayer by a state or the functional equivalent of a state.

_________ are also imposed by many subnational entities. _________ consist of direct tax or indirect tax, and may be paid in money or as its labour equivalent (often but not always unpaid.)

a. 130-30 fund
b. 1921 recession
c. 100-year flood
d. Taxes

17. In economics, _________ is the total supply of goods and services produced by a national economy during a specific time period. It is the total amount of goods and services in the economy available at all possible price levels.

a. Aggregate supply
b. Aggregation problem
c. Aggregate expenditure
d. Aggregate demand

18. In economics, _________ is the ratio of the percent change in one variable to the percent change in another variable. It is a tool for measuring the responsiveness of a function to changes in parameters in a relative way. Commonly analyzed are _________ of substitution, price and wealth.

a. ACEA agreement
b. ACCRA Cost of Living Index
c. Elasticity of demand
d. Elasticity

19. _________ is a broad label that refers to any individuals or households that use goods and services generated within the economy. The concept of a _________ is used in different contexts, so that the usage and significance of the term may vary.

Typically when business people and economists talk of _________s they are talking about person as _________, an aggregated commodity item with little individuality other than that expressed in the buy/not-buy decision.

a. 1921 recession
b. 130-30 fund
c. 100-year flood
d. Consumer

20. Price _________ is defined as the measure of responsiveness in the quantity demanded for a commodity as a result of change in price of the same commodity. It is a measure of how consumers react to a change in price. In other words, it is percentage change in quantity demanded by the percentage change in price of the same commodity.

a. ACEA agreement
b. Elasticity of demand
c. Elasticity
d. ACCRA Cost of Living Index

21. _________ is defined as the measure of responsiveness in the quantity demanded for a commodity as a result of change in price of the same commodity. It is a measure of how consumers react to a change in price. In other words, it is percentage change in quantity demanded as per the percentage change in price of the same commodity.

a. Price elasticity of demand
b. 100-year flood
c. 1921 recession
d. 130-30 fund

22. In economics, the _________ can be defined as the graph depicting the relationship between the price of a certain commodity, and the amount of it that consumers are willing and able to purchase at that given price. It is a graphic representation of a demand schedule. The _________ for all consumers together follows from the _________ of every individual consumer: the individual demands at each price are added together.

a. Kuznets curve
b. Wage curve
c. Cost curve
d. Demand curve

23. In algebra, a _________ is a function depending on n that associates a scalar, det(A), to an n×n square matrix A. The fundamental geometric meaning of a _________ is a scale factor for measure when A is regarded as a linear transformation. _________s are important both in calculus, where they enter the substitution rule for several variables, and in multilinear algebra.

For a fixed nonnegative integer n, there is a unique _________ function for the n×n matrices over any commutative ring R. In particular, this function exists when R is the field of real or complex numbers.

a. 130-30 fund
b. 1921 recession
c. 100-year flood
d. Determinant

24. In mathematics, a _________ is a constant multiplicative factor of a certain object. For example, in the expression $9x^2$, the _________ of $x^2$ is 9.

The object can be such things as a variable, a vector, a function, etc.

a. 130-30 fund
b. 1921 recession
c. 100-year flood
d. Coefficient

25. In economics, _________ describes demand that is not very sensitive to a change in price.
a. Export-led growth
b. Inflation hedge
c. Inelastic
d. Effective unemployment rate

26. _________ is the total money received from the sale of any given quantity of output.

The _________ is calculated by taking the price of the sale times the quantity sold, i.e.

_________ = price X quantity.

.

a. Small numbers game
b. Ceteris paribus
c. Total revenue
d. Market development funds

27. Unemployment occurs when a person is available to work and seeking work but currently without work. The prevalence of unemployment is usually measured using the _________, which is defined as the percentage of those in the labor force who are unemployed. The _________ is also used in economic studies and economic indexes such as the United States' Conference Board's Index of Leading Indicators as a measure of the state of the macroeconomics.
a. ACEA agreement
b. ACCRA Cost of Living Index
c. AD-IA Model
d. Unemployment rate

28. The term '_________' refers to the concept of collecting information and attempting to spot a pattern in the information. In some fields of study, the term '_________' has more formally-defined meanings.

In project management _________ is a mathematical technique that uses historical results to predict future outcome.

a. Quantile regression
b. Coefficient of determination
c. Trend analysis
d. Probit model

29. In economics, the _________ is defined as a numerical measure of the responsiveness of the quantity supplied of product (A) to a change in price of product (A) alone. It is the measure of the way quantity supplied reacts to a change in price.

>

For example, if, in response to a 10% rise in the price of a good, the quantity supplied increases by 20%, the _________ would be 20%/10% = 2.

a. Passive income
b. Price elasticity of supply
c. Demand shaping
d. Hedonimetry

1. _________ is an economic system in which wealth, and the means of producing wealth, are privately owned. Through _________, the land, labor, and capital are owned, operated, and traded for the purpose of generating profits, without force or fraud, by private individuals either singly or jointly, and investments, distribution, income, production, pricing and supply of goods, commodities and services are determined by voluntary private decision in a market economy. A distinguishing feature of _________ is that each person owns his or her own labor and therefore is allowed to sell the use of it to employers.

a. Creative capitalism
b. Socialism for the rich and capitalism for the poor
c. Late capitalism
d. Capitalism

2. _________ is a term that refers both to:

- a formal discipline used to help appraise, or assess, the case for a project or proposal, which itself is a process known as project appraisal; and
- an informal approach to making decisions of any kind.

Under both definitions the process involves, whether explicitly or implicitly, weighing the total expected costs against the total expected benefits of one or more actions in order to choose the best or most profitable option. The formal process is often referred to as either CBA (_________) or BCost-benefit analysis

A hallmark of CBA is that all benefits and all costs are expressed in money terms, and are adjusted for the time value of money, so that all flows of benefits and flows of project costs over time (which tend to occur at different points in time) are expressed on a common basis in terms of their e;present value.e; Closely related, but slightly different, formal techniques include Cost-effectiveness analysis, Economic impact analysis, Fiscal impact analysis and Social Return on Investment(SROI) analysis. The latter builds upon the logic of _________, but differs in that it is explicitly designed to inform the practical decision-making of enterprise managers and investors focused on optimising their social and environmental impacts.

a. 100-year flood
b. 130-30 fund
c. Decision theory
d. Cost-benefit analysis

3. In economics and finance, _________ is the change in total cost that arises when the quantity produced changes by one unit. It is the cost of producing one more unit of a good. Mathematically, the _________ function is expressed as the first derivative of the total cost (TC) function with respect to quantity (Q.)

a. Variable cost
b. Khozraschyot
c. Quality costs
d. Marginal cost

4. In microeconomics, _________ is the extra revenue that an additional unit of product will bring. It is the additional income from selling one more unit of a good; sometimes equal to price. It can also be described as the change in total revenue/change in number of units sold.

a. Market demand schedule
b. Reservation price
c. Long term
d. Marginal revenue

5. _________ or economic opportunity loss is the value of the next best alternative foregone as the result of making a decision. _________ analysis is an important part of a company's decision-making processes but is not treated as an actual cost in any financial statement. The next best thing that a person can engage in is referred to as the _________ of doing the best thing and ignoring the next best thing to be done.

a. Industrial organization
b. Economic
c. Economic ideology
d. Opportunity cost

6. In microeconomics, _________ is quite simply the conversion of inputs into outputs. It is an economic process that uses resources to create a good or service that is suitable for exchange. This can include manufacturing, storing, shipping, and packaging.

a. MET
b. Red Guards
c. Solved
d. Production

7. An _________ is an easy accounted cost, such as wage, rent and materials. It can be transacted in the form of money payment and is lost directly, as opposed to monetary implicit costs.

a. Explicit cost
b. Inventory valuation
c. Average variable cost
d. Average fixed cost

8. In economics, an _________ occurs when one foregoes an alternative action but does not make an actual payment. (For instance, the explicit cost of a night at the movies includes the moviegoer's ticket and soda, but the _________ includes the pay he would have earned if he had chosen to work instead.) _________s are related to forgone benefits of any single transaction.

a. External sector
b. Ostrich strategy
c. Overnight trade
d. Implicit cost

9. In economics, _________ are business expenses that are not dependent on the activities of the business They tend to be time-related, such as salaries or rents being paid per month. This is in contrast to variable costs, which are volume-related (and are paid per quantity.)

In management accounting, _________ are defined as expenses that do not change in proportion to the activity of a business, within the relevant period or scale of production.

a. Cost of poor quality
b. Fixed costs
c. Cost-Volume-Profit Analysis
d. Quality costs

10. _________s are expenses that change in proportion to the activity of a business. In other words, _________ is the sum of marginal costs. It can also be considered normal costs.

a. Cost-Volume-Profit Analysis
b. Quality costs
c. Variable cost
d. Cost allocation

11. In economics and business decision-making, _________ are costs that cannot be recovered once they have been incurred. _________ are sometimes contrasted with variable costs, which are the costs that will change due to the proposed course of action, and prospective costs which are costs that will be incurred if an action is taken.

In traditional microeconomic theory, only variable costs are relevant to a decision.

a. Halo effect
b. Sunk costs
c. Hyperbolic discounting
d. Post-purchase rationalization

12. _________ in economics refers to metrics and measures of output from production processes, per unit of input. Labor _________, for example, is typically measured as a ratio of output per labor-hour, an input. _________ may be conceived of as a metrics of the technical or engineering efficiency of production.

a. Productivity
b. Production-possibility frontier
c. Fordism
d. Piece work

13. In economics, and cost accounting, _________ describes the total economic cost of production and is made up of variable costs, which vary according to the quantity of a good produced and include inputs such as labor and raw materials, plus fixed costs, which are independent of the quantity of a good produced and include inputs (capital) that cannot be varied in the short term, such as buildings and machinery. _________ in economics includes the total opportunity cost of each factor of production in addition to fixed and variable costs.

The rate at which _________ changes as the amount produced changes is called marginal cost.

a. Total cost
b. 100-year flood
c. 1921 recession
d. 130-30 fund

14. _________ is the total money received from the sale of any given quantity of output.

The _________ is calculated by taking the price of the sale times the quantity sold, i.e.

_________ = price X quantity.

.

a. Market development funds
b. Ceteris paribus
c. Small numbers game
d. Total revenue

15. In economics, _________ is a measure of the relative satisfaction from consumption of various goods and services. Given this measure, one may speak meaningfully of increasing or decreasing _________, and thereby explain economic behavior in terms of attempts to increase one's _________. For illustrative purposes, changes in _________ are sometimes expressed in units called utils.

a. Utility function
b. Expected utility hypothesis
c. Ordinal utility
d. Utility

16. In economics and especially in the theory of competition, _________ are obstacles in the path of a firm that make it difficult to enter a given market.

_________ are the source of a firm's pricing power - the ability of a firm to raise prices without losing all its customers.

The term refers to hindrances that an individual may face while trying to gain entrance into a profession or trade.

a. Group boycott
b. Limit price
c. Social dumping
d. Barriers to entry

17. In economics, _________ is the ratio of the percent change in one variable to the percent change in another variable. It is a tool for measuring the responsiveness of a function to changes in parameters in a relative way. Commonly analyzed are _________ of substitution, price and wealth.

a. ACEA agreement
b. Elasticity of demand
c. ACCRA Cost of Living Index
d. Elasticity

18. _________ is a fee paid on borrowed assets. It is the price paid for the use of borrowed money , or, money earned by deposited funds . Assets that are sometimes lent with _________ include money, shares, consumer goods through hire purchase, major assets such as aircraft, and even entire factories in finance lease arrangements.

a. Asset protection
b. Interest
c. Insolvency
d. Internal debt

19. An _________ is the price a borrower pays for the use of money they do not own, for instance a small company might borrow from a bank to kick start their business, and the return a lender receives for deferring the use of funds, by lending it to the borrower. _________s are normally expressed as a percentage rate over the period of one year.

_________s targets are also a vital tool of monetary policy and are used to control variables like investment, inflation, and unemployment.

a. Enterprise value
b. Arrow-Debreu model
c. Interest rate
d. ACCRA Cost of Living Index

20. In economics, the concept of the _________ refers to the decision-making time frame of a firm in which at least one factor of production is fixed. Costs which are fixed in the _________ have no impact on a firms decisions. For example a firm can raise output by increasing the amount of labour through overtime.

a. Short-run
b. Hicks-neutral technical change
c. Product Pipeline
d. Productivity model

21. _________ is an economics term used to describe the total fixed costs (TFC) divided by the quantity (Q) of units produced.

$$AFC = \frac{TFC}{Q}$$

_________ is a per-unit measure of fixed costs. As the total number of goods produced increases, the _________ decreases because the same amount of fixed costs are being spread over a larger number of units.

a. Inventory valuation
b. Average fixed cost
c. Average variable cost
d. Explicit cost

22. _________ is an economics term to describe a firms variable costs (labor, electricity, etc.) divided by the quantity (Q) of total units of output.

$$AVC = \frac{TVC}{Q}$$

Where:

- TVC = Total Variable Cost
- _________ = Average variable cost
- Q = Quantity of Units Produced

_________ plus average fixed cost equals average total cost:

_________ + AFC = ATC.

.

a. Inventory valuation
b. Average variable cost
c. Explicit cost
d. Average fixed cost

23. In economics, a _________ is a graph of the costs of production as a function of total quantity produced. In a free market economy, productively efficient firms use these curves to find the optimal point of production, where they make the most profits. There are a few different types of _________s, each relevant to a different area of economics.

a. Phillips curve
b. Demand curve
c. Cost curve
d. Kuznets curve

24. In economics, _________ is the total demand for final goods and services in the economy (Y) at a given time and price level. It is the amount of goods and services in the economy that will be purchased at all possible price levels. This is the demand for the gross domestic product of a country when inventory levels are static.

a. Aggregate demand
b. Aggregation problem
c. Aggregate supply
d. Aggregate expenditure

25. Economics:

- _________,the desire to own something and the ability to pay for it
- _________ curve,a graphic representation of a _________ schedule
- _________ deposit, the money in checking accounts
- _________ pull theory,the theory that inflation occurs when _________ for goods and services exceeds existing supplies
- _________ schedule,a table that lists the quantity of a good a person will buy it each different price
- _________ side economics,the school of economics at believes government spending and tax cuts open economy by raising _________

.

a. McKesson ' Robbins scandal
b. Variability
c. Production
d. Demand

26. In economics, _________ is the process by which a firm determines the price and output level that returns the greatest profit. There are several approaches to this problem. The total revenue--total cost method relies on the fact that profit equals revenue minus cost, and the marginal revenue--marginal cost method is based on the fact that total profit in a perfectly competitive market reaches its maximum point where marginal revenue equals marginal cost.

a. Profit maximization
b. 100-year flood
c. Normal profit
d. Profit margin

1. In economics, _________ is the total demand for final goods and services in the economy (Y) at a given time and price level. It is the amount of goods and services in the economy that will be purchased at all possible price levels. This is the demand for the gross domestic product of a country when inventory levels are static.

a. Aggregate supply
b. Aggregation problem
c. Aggregate expenditure
d. Aggregate demand

2. Economics:

- _________,the desire to own something and the ability to pay for it
- _________ curve,a graphic representation of a _________ schedule
- _________ deposit, the money in checking accounts
- _________ pull theory,the theory that inflation occurs when _________ for goods and services exceeds existing supplies
- _________ schedule,a table that lists the quantity of a good a person will buy it each different price
- _________ side economics,the school of economics at believes government spending and tax cuts open economy by raising _________

.

a. McKesson ' Robbins scandal
b. Variability
c. Production
d. Demand

3. _________ is an economic system in which wealth, and the means of producing wealth, are privately owned. Through _________, the land, labor, and capital are owned, operated, and traded for the purpose of generating profits, without force or fraud, by private individuals either singly or jointly, and investments, distribution, income, production, pricing and supply of goods, commodities and services are determined by voluntary private decision in a market economy. A distinguishing feature of _________ is that each person owns his or her own labor and therefore is allowed to sell the use of it to employers.

a. Socialism for the rich and capitalism for the poor
b. Capitalism
c. Late capitalism
d. Creative capitalism

4. _________ in economics and business is the result of an exchange and from that trade we assign a numerical monetary value to a good, service or asset. If Alice trades Bob 4 apples for an orange, the _________ of an orange is 4 apples. Inversely, the _________ of an apple is 1/4 oranges.

a. Premium pricing
b. Price war
c. Price book
d. Price

5. Monopoly power is an example of market failure which occurs when one or more of the participants has the ability to influence the price or other outcomes in some general or specialized market. The most commonly discussed form of market power is that of a monopoly, but other forms such as monopsony, and more moderate versions of these two extremes, exist. Market participants that have market power are sometimes referred to as 'price makers', while those without are sometimes called '_________'.

a. Market power
b. Price takers
c. Market concentration
d. Monopolization

6. In economics, the _________ can be defined as the graph depicting the relationship between the price of a certain commodity, and the amount of it that consumers are willing and able to purchase at that given price. It is a graphic representation of a demand schedule. The _________ for all consumers together follows from the _________ of every individual consumer: the individual demands at each price are added together.

a. Wage curve
b. Kuznets curve
c. Cost curve
d. Demand curve

7. In economics, _________ is the process by which a firm determines the price and output level that returns the greatest profit. There are several approaches to this problem. The total revenue--total cost method relies on the fact that profit equals revenue minus cost, and the marginal revenue--marginal cost method is based on the fact that total profit in a perfectly competitive market reaches its maximum point where marginal revenue equals marginal cost.

a. Profit margin
b. Profit maximization
c. 100-year flood
d. Normal profit

8. In economics and finance, _________ is the change in total cost that arises when the quantity produced changes by one unit. It is the cost of producing one more unit of a good. Mathematically, the _________ function is expressed as the first derivative of the total cost (TC) function with respect to quantity (Q.)

a. Quality costs
b. Marginal cost
c. Khozraschyot
d. Variable cost

9. In microeconomics, _________ is the extra revenue that an additional unit of product will bring. It is the additional income from selling one more unit of a good; sometimes equal to price. It can also be described as the change in total revenue/change in number of units sold.

a. Market demand schedule
b. Long term
c. Reservation price
d. Marginal revenue

10. _________ in economics refers to metrics and measures of output from production processes, per unit of input. Labor _________, for example, is typically measured as a ratio of output per labor-hour, an input. _________ may be conceived of as a metrics of the technical or engineering efficiency of production.

a. Fordism
b. Productivity
c. Piece work
d. Production-possibility frontier

11. In economics, the concept of the _________ refers to the decision-making time frame of a firm in which at least one factor of production is fixed. Costs which are fixed in the _________ have no impact on a firms decisions. For example a firm can raise output by increasing the amount of labour through overtime.

a. Hicks-neutral technical change
b. Product Pipeline
c. Productivity model
d. Short-run

12. _________s is the social science that studies the production, distribution, and consumption of goods and services. The term _________s comes from the Ancient Greek oá¼°κονομῖα from oá¼¶κος (oikos, 'house') + vÏŒμος (nomos, 'custom' or 'law'), hence 'rules of the house(hold)'. Current _________ models developed out of the broader field of political economy in the late 19th century, owing to a desire to use an empirical approach more akin to the physical sciences.

a. Energy economics
b. Inflation
c. Economic
d. Opportunity cost

13. In economics, _________ is the difference between a company's total revenue and its opportunity costs. It is the increase in wealth that an investor has from making an investment, taking into consideration all costs associated with that investment including the opportunity cost of capital.

Profit is the factor income of the entrepreneur.

a. ACCRA Cost of Living Index
b. Economic profit
c. Accounting profit
d. Operating profit

14. An _________ is an easy accounted cost, such as wage, rent and materials. It can be transacted in the form of money payment and is lost directly, as opposed to monetary implicit costs.
a. Inventory valuation
b. Average variable cost
c. Explicit cost
d. Average fixed cost

15. In economics, an _________ occurs when one foregoes an alternative action but does not make an actual payment. (For instance, the explicit cost of a night at the movies includes the moviegoer's ticket and soda, but the _________ includes the pay he would have earned if he had chosen to work instead.) _________s are related to forgone benefits of any single transaction.
a. Implicit cost
b. Overnight trade
c. External sector
d. Ostrich strategy

16. _________ is a component of the firm's opportunity costs. The time that the owner spends running the firm could be spent on running another firm. This is _________: the return the entrepreneur can expect to earn or the profit that the business owners considers necessary to make running the business worth his/her while.
a. Profit margin
b. 100-year flood
c. Profit maximization
d. Normal profit

17. In economics and business, specifically cost accounting, the _________ point (BEP) is the point at which cost or expenses and revenue are equal: there is no net loss or gain, and one has 'broken even'. A profit or a loss has not been made, although opportunity costs have been paid, and capital has received the risk-adjusted, expected return.

For example, if the business sells less than 200 tables each month, it will make a loss, if it sells more, it will be a profit.

a. Nonmarket
b. Small numbers game
c. Buffer stock scheme
d. Break-even

18. In economics and especially in the theory of competition, _________ are obstacles in the path of a firm that make it difficult to enter a given market.

_________ are the source of a firm's pricing power - the ability of a firm to raise prices without losing all its customers.

The term refers to hindrances that an individual may face while trying to gain entrance into a profession or trade.

a. Limit price
b. Group boycott
c. Social dumping
d. Barriers to entry

19. _________ is a fee paid on borrowed assets. It is the price paid for the use of borrowed money , or, money earned by deposited funds . Assets that are sometimes lent with _________ include money, shares, consumer goods through hire purchase, major assets such as aircraft, and even entire factories in finance lease arrangements.

a. Insolvency
b. Interest
c. Asset protection
d. Internal debt

20. An _________ is the price a borrower pays for the use of money they do not own, for instance a small company might borrow from a bank to kick start their business, and the return a lender receives for deferring the use of funds, by lending it to the borrower. _________s are normally expressed as a percentage rate over the period of one year.

_________s targets are also a vital tool of monetary policy and are used to control variables like investment, inflation, and unemployment.

a. Enterprise value
b. Interest rate
c. ACCRA Cost of Living Index
d. Arrow-Debreu model

21. In economic models, the _________ time frame assumes no fixed factors of production. Firms can enter or leave the marketplace, and the cost (and availability) of land, labor, raw materials, and capital goods can be assumed to vary. In contrast, in the short-run time frame, certain factors are assumed to be fixed, because there is not sufficient time for them to change.

a. Price/performance ratio
b. Productivity world
c. Diseconomies of scale
d. Long-run

22. _________ is used to refer to a number of related concepts. It is the using resources in such a way as to maximize the production of goods and services. A system can be called economically efficient if:

- No one can be made better off without making someone else worse off.
- More output cannot be obtained without increasing the amount of inputs.
- Production proceeds at the lowest possible per-unit cost.

These definitions of efficiency are not equivalent, but they are all encompassed by the idea that nothing more can be achieved given the resources available.

An economic system is more efficient if it can provide more goods and services for society without using more resources.

a. ACEA agreement
b. ACCRA Cost of Living Index
c. Efficient contract theory
d. Economic efficiency

23. In microeconomics, _________ is quite simply the conversion of inputs into outputs. It is an economic process that uses resources to create a good or service that is suitable for exchange. This can include manufacturing, storing, shipping, and packaging.

a. Red Guards
b. Production
c. Solved
d. MET

24. In economics _________ is defined as the sum of private and external costs. Economic theorists ascribe individual decision-making to a calculation costs and benefits. Rational choice theory assumes that individuals only consider their own private costs when making decisions, not the costs that may be borne by others.

a. Psychic cost
b. Cost-Volume-Profit Analysis
c. Khozraschyot
d. Social cost

1. In economics, _________ is the ability of a firm to alter the market price of a good or service. A firm with _________ can raise prices without losing all customers to competitors.

When a firm has _________ it faces a downward-sloping demand curve.

a. Price makers
b. Pacman conjecture
c. Revenue-cap regulation
d. Market power

2. _________ in economics and business is the result of an exchange and from that trade we assign a numerical monetary value to a good, service or asset. If Alice trades Bob 4 apples for an orange, the _________ of an orange is 4 apples. Inversely, the _________ of an apple is 1/4 oranges.

a. Price book
b. Price
c. Premium pricing
d. Price war

3. Monopoly power is an example of market failure which occurs when one or more of the participants has the ability to influence the price or other outcomes in some general or specialized market. The most commonly discussed form of market power is that of a monopoly, but other forms such as monopsony, and more moderate versions of these two extremes, exist. Market participants that have market power are sometimes referred to as 'price makers', while those without are sometimes called '_________'.

a. Market concentration
b. Market power
c. Monopolization
d. Price takers

4. In marketing, _________ is the process of distinguishing the differences of a product or offering from others, to make it more attractive to a particular target market. This involves differentiating it from competitors' products as well as one's own product offerings.

Differentiation is a source of competitive advantage.

a. Pricing science
b. Market segment
c. Technology acceptance model
d. Product differentiation

5. A _________ is a counterfeit agreement among industries. It is an informal organization of producers that agree to coordinate prices and production. _________s usually occur in an oligopolistic industry, where there is a small number of sellers and usually involve homogeneous products.

a. Cartel
b. 100-year flood
c. Shill
d. Shanzhai

6. _________ is the transition of a national economy from monopoly control by groups of large businesses to a free market economy. This change rarely arises naturally, and is generally the result of regulation by a governing body.

A modern example of _________ is the economic restructuring of Germany after the fall of the Third Reich in 1945.

a. Market power
b. Monopolization
c. Decartelization
d. Complementary monopoly

7. The _________ consists of a number of economic theories which describe the nature of the firm, company including its existence, its behaviour, and its relationship with the market.

In simplified terms, the _________ aims to answer these questions:

1. Existence - why do firms emerge, why are not all transactions in the economy mediated over the market?
2. Boundaries - why the boundary between firms and the market is located exactly there? Which transactions are performed internally and which are negotiated on the market?
3. Organization - why are firms structured in such specific way? What is the interplay of formal and informal relationships?

Despite looking simple, these questions are not answered by the established economic theory, which usually views firms as given, and treats them as black boxes without any internal structure.

The First World War period saw a change of emphasis in economic theory away from industry-level analysis which mainly included analysing markets to analysis at the level of the firm, as it became increasingly clear that perfect competition was no longer an adequate model of how firms behaved. Economic theory till then had focussed on trying to understand markets alone and there had been little study on understanding why firms or organisations exist.

a. Theory of the firm
b. Technology gap
c. Policy Ineffectiveness Proposition
d. Khazzoom-Brookes postulate

8. Economics:

- _________,the desire to own something and the ability to pay for it
- _________ curve,a graphic representation of a _________ schedule
- _________ deposit, the money in checking accounts
- _________ pull theory,the theory that inflation occurs when _________ for goods and services exceeds existing supplies
- _________ schedule,a table that lists the quantity of a good a person will buy it each different price
- _________ side economics,the school of economics at believes government spending and tax cuts open economy by raising _________

.

a. Demand
b. Variability
c. McKesson ' Robbins scandal
d. Production

9. In economics, the _________ can be defined as the graph depicting the relationship between the price of a certain commodity, and the amount of it that consumers are willing and able to purchase at that given price. It is a graphic representation of a demand schedule. The _________ for all consumers together follows from the _________ of every individual consumer: the individual demands at each price are added together.

a. Wage curve
b. Kuznets curve
c. Cost curve
d. Demand curve

10. In economics, _________ describes demand that is not very sensitive to a change in price.

a. Inflation hedge
b. Export-led growth
c. Effective unemployment rate
d. Inelastic

11. _________, in microeconomics, are the cost advantages that a business obtains due to expansion. They are factors that cause a producere;s average cost per unit to fall as scale is increased. _________ is a long run concept and refers to reductions in unit cost as the size of a facility, or scale, increases.

a. Economic production quantity
b. Isoquant
c. Underinvestment employment relationship
d. Economies of scale

12. In economics and especially in the theory of competition, _________ are obstacles in the path of a firm that make it difficult to enter a given market.

_________ are the source of a firm's pricing power - the ability of a firm to raise prices without losing all its customers.

The term refers to hindrances that an individual may face while trying to gain entrance into a profession or trade.

a. Social dumping
b. Group boycott
c. Limit price
d. Barriers to entry

13. In economics, _________ is the process by which a firm determines the price and output level that returns the greatest profit. There are several approaches to this problem. The total revenue--total cost method relies on the fact that profit equals revenue minus cost, and the marginal revenue--marginal cost method is based on the fact that total profit in a perfectly competitive market reaches its maximum point where marginal revenue equals marginal cost.

a. Profit margin
b. Normal profit
c. 100-year flood
d. Profit maximization

14. A _________ is:

- Rewrite _________, in generative grammar and computer science
- Standardization, a formal and widely-accepted statement, fact, definition, or qualification
- Operation, a determinate _________ for performing a mathematical operation and obtaining a certain result (Mathematics, Logic)
    - Unary operation
    - Binary operation
- _________ of inference, a function from sets of formulae to formulae (Mathematics, Logic)
- _________ of thumb, principle with broad application that is not intended to be strictly accurate or reliable for every situation. Also often simply referred to as a _________
- Moral, an atomic element of a moral code for guiding choices in human behavior
- Heuristic, a quantized '_________' which shows a tendency or probability for successful function
- A regulation, as in sports
- A Production _________, as in computer science
- Procedural law, a _________set governing the application of laws to cases
    - A law, which may informally be called a '_________'
    - A court ruling, a decision by a court
- In the U.S. Government, a regulation mandated by Congress, but written or expanded upon by the Executive Branch.
- Norm (sociology), an informal but widely accepted _________, concept, truth, definition, or qualification (social norms, legal norms, coding norms)
- Norm (philosophy), a kind of sentence or a reason to act, feel or believe
- 'Rulership' is the concept of governance by a government:
    - Military _________, governance by a military body
    - Monastic _________, a collection of precepts that guides the life of monks or nuns in a religious order where the superior holds the place of Christ
- Slide _________

- '_________,' a song by Ayumi Hamasaki
- '_________,' a song by rapper Nas
- '_________s,' an album by the band The Whitest Boy Alive
- _________s: Pyaar Ka Superhit Formula, a 2003 Bollywood film
- ruler, an instrument for measuring lengths
- _________, a component of an astrolabe, circumferator or similar instrument
- The _________s, a bestselling self-help book
- _________ Project (Run Up-to-date Linux Everywhere), a project that aims to use up-to-date Linux software on old PCs
- _________ engine, a software system that helps managing business _________s
- Ja _________, a hip hop artist
    - R.U.L.E., a 2005 greatest hits album by rapper Ja _________
- '_________s,' a KMFDM song

a. Technocracy
b. Rule
c. Demand
d. Procter ' Gamble

15. In microeconomics, _________ is the extra revenue that an additional unit of product will bring. It is the additional income from selling one more unit of a good; sometimes equal to price. It can also be described as the change in total revenue/change in number of units sold.

a. Reservation price
b. Long term
c. Marginal revenue
d. Market demand schedule

16. In economics and finance, _________ is the change in total cost that arises when the quantity produced changes by one unit. It is the cost of producing one more unit of a good. Mathematically, the _________ function is expressed as the first derivative of the total cost (TC) function with respect to quantity (Q.)

a. Khozraschyot
b. Marginal cost
c. Variable cost
d. Quality costs

17. _________ exists when sales of identical goods or services are transacted at different prices from the same provider. In a theoretical market with perfect information, no transaction costs or prohibition on secondary exchange (or re-selling) to prevent arbitrage, _________ can only be a feature of monopoly and oligopoly markets, where market power can be exercised. Otherwise, the moment the seller tries to sell the same good at different prices, the buyer at the lower price can arbitrage by selling to the consumer buying at the higher price but with a tiny discount.

a. Loss leader
b. Transfer pricing
c. Lerner Index
d. Price discrimination

18. _________ in economics refers to metrics and measures of output from production processes, per unit of input. Labor _________, for example, is typically measured as a ratio of output per labor-hour, an input. _________ may be conceived of as a metrics of the technical or engineering efficiency of production.

a. Piece work
b. Production-possibility frontier
c. Fordism
d. Productivity

19. In economics, the concept of the _________ refers to the decision-making time frame of a firm in which at least one factor of production is fixed. Costs which are fixed in the _________ have no impact on a firms decisions. For example a firm can raise output by increasing the amount of labour through overtime.

a. Productivity model
b. Hicks-neutral technical change
c. Product Pipeline
d. Short-run

20. In economic models, the _________ time frame assumes no fixed factors of production. Firms can enter or leave the marketplace, and the cost (and availability) of land, labor, raw materials, and capital goods can be assumed to vary. In contrast, in the short-run time frame, certain factors are assumed to be fixed, because there is not sufficient time for them to change.

a. Productivity world
b. Long-run
c. Diseconomies of scale
d. Price/performance ratio

21. _________ is used to assign the available resources in an economic way. It is part of resource management.

In strategic planning,is a plan for using available resources, for example human resources, especially in the near term, to achieve goals for the future.

a. 1921 recession
b. 100-year flood
c. 130-30 fund
d. Resource allocation

22. In economics, an externality or spillover of an economic transaction is an impact on a party that is not directly involved in the transaction. In such a case, prices do not reflect the full costs or benefits in production or consumption of a product or service. A positive impact is called an _________, while a negative impact is called an external cost.

a. ACEA agreement
b. AD-IA Model
c. ACCRA Cost of Living Index
d. External benefit

23. _________s is the social science that studies the production, distribution, and consumption of goods and services. The term _________s comes from the Ancient Greek oá¼°κονομÎ¯α from oá¼¶κος (oikos, 'house') + vÏŒμος (nomos, 'custom' or 'law'), hence 'rules of the house(hold)'. Current _________ models developed out of the broader field of political economy in the late 19th century, owing to a desire to use an empirical approach more akin to the physical sciences.

a. Economic
b. Energy economics
c. Inflation
d. Opportunity cost

24. _________ is used to refer to a number of related concepts. It is the using resources in such a way as to maximize the production of goods and services. A system can be called economically efficient if:

- No one can be made better off without making someone else worse off.
- More output cannot be obtained without increasing the amount of inputs.
- Production proceeds at the lowest possible per-unit cost.

These definitions of efficiency are not equivalent, but they are all encompassed by the idea that nothing more can be achieved given the resources available.

An economic system is more efficient if it can provide more goods and services for society without using more resources.

a. Economic efficiency
b. ACEA agreement
c. Efficient contract theory
d. ACCRA Cost of Living Index

25. In economics, a _________ is a graph of the costs of production as a function of total quantity produced. In a free market economy, productively efficient firms use these curves to find the optimal point of production, where they make the most profits. There are a few different types of _________s, each relevant to a different area of economics.

a. Phillips curve
b. Kuznets curve
c. Demand curve
d. Cost curve

26. In economics, and cost accounting, _________ describes the total economic cost of production and is made up of variable costs, which vary according to the quantity of a good produced and include inputs such as labor and raw materials, plus fixed costs, which are independent of the quantity of a good produced and include inputs (capital) that cannot be varied in the short term, such as buildings and machinery. _________ in economics includes the total opportunity cost of each factor of production in addition to fixed and variable costs.

The rate at which _________ changes as the amount produced changes is called marginal cost.

a. 100-year flood
b. 130-30 fund
c. 1921 recession
d. Total cost

27. _________ are the forces that cause larger firms to produce goods and services at increased per-unit costs. They are less well known than what economists have long understood as 'economies of scale', the forces which enable larger firms to produce goods and services at reduced per-unit costs.

Some of the forces which cause a diseconomy of scale are listed below:

Ideally, all employees of a firm would have one-on-one communication with each other so they know exactly what the other workers are doing.

a. Productive capacity
b. Diseconomies of scale
c. Factors of production
d. Marginal physical product

28. _________ is a pricing method used by companies. It is used primarily because it is easy to calculate and requires little information. There are several varieties, but the common thread in all of them is that one first calculates the cost of the product, then includes an additional amount to represent profit.

a. Target costing
b. Rational pricing
c. Best available rate
d. Cost-plus pricing

29. In economics, _________ is the total demand for final goods and services in the economy (Y) at a given time and price level. It is the amount of goods and services in the economy that will be purchased at all possible price levels. This is the demand for the gross domestic product of a country when inventory levels are static.

a. Aggregate expenditure
b. Aggregate supply
c. Aggregation problem
d. Aggregate demand

30. _________ is one of the four Ps of the marketing mix. The other three aspects are product, promotion, and place. It is also a key variable in microeconomic price allocation theory.

a. Premium pricing
b. Pricing
c. Guaranteed Maximum Price
d. Point of total assumption

1. _________ is a common market structure where many competing producers sell products that are differentiated from one another (ie. the products are substitutes, but are not exactly alike.) Many markets are monopolistically competitive, common examples include the markets for restaurants, cereal, clothing, shoes and service industries in large cities.

a. Monopolistic competition
b. Financial crisis
c. Perfect competition
d. Mathematical economics

2. _________ is an economic system in which wealth, and the means of producing wealth, are privately owned. Through _________, the land, labor, and capital are owned, operated, and traded for the purpose of generating profits, without force or fraud, by private individuals either singly or jointly, and investments, distribution, income, production, pricing and supply of goods, commodities and services are determined by voluntary private decision in a market economy. A distinguishing feature of _________ is that each person owns his or her own labor and therefore is allowed to sell the use of it to employers.

a. Late capitalism
b. Creative capitalism
c. Capitalism
d. Socialism for the rich and capitalism for the poor

3. _________, in microeconomics, are the cost advantages that a business obtains due to expansion. They are factors that cause a producere;s average cost per unit to fall as scale is increased. _________ is a long run concept and refers to reductions in unit cost as the size of a facility, or scale, increases.

a. Economies of scale
b. Economic production quantity
c. Underinvestment employment relationship
d. Isoquant

4. A _________ is a counterfeit agreement among industries. It is an informal organization of producers that agree to coordinate prices and production. _________s usually occur in an oligopolistic industry, where there is a small number of sellers and usually involve homogeneous products.

a. 100-year flood
b. Cartel
c. Shill
d. Shanzhai

5. In economics, _________ is the ability of a firm to alter the market price of a good or service. A firm with _________ can raise prices without losing all customers to competitors.

When a firm has _________ it faces a downward-sloping demand curve.

a. Revenue-cap regulation
b. Market power
c. Pacman conjecture
d. Price makers

6. In economic models, the _________ time frame assumes no fixed factors of production. Firms can enter or leave the marketplace, and the cost (and availability) of land, labor, raw materials, and capital goods can be assumed to vary. In contrast, in the short-run time frame, certain factors are assumed to be fixed, because there is not sufficient time for them to change.

a. Diseconomies of scale
b. Price/performance ratio
c. Productivity world
d. Long-run

7. _________ is used to assign the available resources in an economic way. It is part of resource management.

In strategic planning,is a plan for using available resources, for example human resources, especially in the near term, to achieve goals for the future.

a. 100-year flood
b. 130-30 fund
c. 1921 recession
d. Resource allocation

8. In economics, an externality or spillover of an economic transaction is an impact on a party that is not directly involved in the transaction. In such a case, prices do not reflect the full costs or benefits in production or consumption of a product or service. A positive impact is called an _________, while a negative impact is called an external cost.

a. ACCRA Cost of Living Index
b. AD-IA Model
c. External benefit
d. ACEA agreement

9. An _________ is a market form in which a market or industry is dominated by a small number of sellers (oligopolists.) Because there are few participants in this type of market, each oligopolist is aware of the actions of the others. The decisions of one firm influence, and are influenced by, the decisions of other firms.

a. Oligopsony
b. ACEA agreement
c. Oligopoly
d. ACCRA Cost of Living Index

10. _________ in economics and business is the result of an exchange and from that trade we assign a numerical monetary value to a good, service or asset. If Alice trades Bob 4 apples for an orange, the _________ of an orange is 4 apples. Inversely, the _________ of an apple is 1/4 oranges.

a. Price book
b. Price war
c. Premium pricing
d. Price

11. In economics and especially in the theory of competition, _________ are obstacles in the path of a firm that make it difficult to enter a given market.

_________ are the source of a firm's pricing power - the ability of a firm to raise prices without losing all its customers.

The term refers to hindrances that an individual may face while trying to gain entrance into a profession or trade.

a. Social dumping
b. Limit price
c. Group boycott
d. Barriers to entry

12. _________ is a branch of applied mathematics that is used in the social sciences (most notably economics), biology, engineering, political science, international relations, computer science, and philosophy. _________ attempts to mathematically capture behavior in strategic situations, in which an individual's success in making choices depends on the choices of others. While initially developed to analyze competitions in which one individual does better at another's expense (zero sum games), it has been expanded to treat a wide class of interactions, which are classified according to several criteria.

a. Dollar auction
b. Proper equilibrium
c. Discriminatory price auction
d. Game theory

13. In marketing, _________ is the process of distinguishing the differences of a product or offering from others, to make it more attractive to a particular target market. This involves differentiating it from competitors' products as well as one's own product offerings.

Differentiation is a source of competitive advantage.

a. Technology acceptance model
b. Pricing science
c. Market segment
d. Product differentiation

14. _________ is an agreement, usually secretive, which occurs between two or more persons to deceive, mislead or to obtain an objective forbidden by law typically involving fraud or gaining an unfair advantage. It is an agreement among firms to divide the market, set prices kickbacks, or misrepresenting the independence of the relationship between the colluding parties.' All acts effected by _________ are considered void.

a. Bid rigging
b. Net Book Agreement
c. Dividing territories
d. Collusion

15. _________ is a term used in competition law to describe price-fixing between competitors in an oligopoly that occurs without an actual spoken agreement between the parties. Instead, one competitor will take the lead in raising prices. The others will then follow suit, raising their prices by the same amount, with the unspoken mutual understanding that all will reap greater profits from the higher prices so long as none attempts to undercut the others.

a. Social dumping
b. Conscious parallelism
c. Group boycott
d. Net Book Agreement

16. In economics, a _________ exists when a specific individual or enterprise has sufficient control over a particular product or service to determine significantly the terms on which other individuals shall have access to it. Monopolies are thus characterized by a lack of economic competition for the good or service that they provide and a lack of viable substitute goods. The verb 'monopolize' refers to the process by which a firm gains persistently greater market share than what is expected under perfect competition.

a. 130-30 fund
b. 100-year flood
c. 1921 recession
d. Monopoly

17. In economics, _________ is the process by which a firm determines the price and output level that returns the greatest profit. There are several approaches to this problem. The total revenue--total cost method relies on the fact that profit equals revenue minus cost, and the marginal revenue--marginal cost method is based on the fact that total profit in a perfectly competitive market reaches its maximum point where marginal revenue equals marginal cost.

a. Profit margin
b. Profit maximization
c. Normal profit
d. 100-year flood

18. Economics:

- _________,the desire to own something and the ability to pay for it
- _________ curve,a graphic representation of a _________ schedule
- _________ deposit, the money in checking accounts
- _________ pull theory,the theory that inflation occurs when _________ for goods and services exceeds existing supplies
- _________ schedule,a table that lists the quantity of a good a person will buy it each different price
- _________ side economics,the school of economics at believes government spending and tax cuts open economy by raising _________

a. McKesson ' Robbins scandal
b. Demand
c. Production
d. Variability

19. In economics, the _________ can be defined as the graph depicting the relationship between the price of a certain commodity, and the amount of it that consumers are willing and able to purchase at that given price. It is a graphic representation of a demand schedule. The _________ for all consumers together follows from the _________ of every individual consumer: the individual demands at each price are added together.

a. Kuznets curve
b. Wage curve
c. Cost curve
d. Demand curve

20. In economics, _________ describes demand that is not very sensitive to a change in price.

a. Inflation hedge
b. Export-led growth
c. Effective unemployment rate
d. Inelastic

21. Competition law, known in the United States as _________ law, has three main elements:

- prohibiting agreements or practices that restrict free trading and competition between business entities. This includes in particular the repression of cartels.
- banning abusive behaviour by a firm dominating a market, or anti-competitive practices that tend to lead to such a dominant position. Practices controlled in this way may include predatory pricing, tying, price gouging, refusal to deal, and many others.
- supervising the mergers and acquisitions of large corporations, including some joint ventures. Transactions that are considered to threaten the competitive process can be prohibited altogether, or approved subject to 'remedies' such as an obligation to divest part of the merged business or to offer licences or access to facilities to enable other businesses to continue competing.

The substance and practice of competition law varies from jurisdiction to jurisdiction. Protecting the interests of consumers (consumer welfare) and ensuring that entrepreneurs have an opportunity to compete in the market economy are often treated as important objectives. Competition law is closely connected with law on deregulation of access to markets, state aids and subsidies, the privatisation of state owned assets and the establishment of independent sector regulators. In recent decades, competition law has been viewed as a way to provide better public services.

a. United Kingdom competition law
b. Anti-Inflation Act
c. Intellectual property law
d. Antitrust

22. The phrase _________ and acquisitions refers to the aspect of corporate strategy, corporate finance and management dealing with the buying, selling and combining of different companies that can aid, finance, or help a growing company in a given industry grow rapidly without having to create another business entity.

An acquisition, also known as a takeover or a buyout, is the buying of one company (the 'target') by another. An acquisition may be friendly or hostile.

a. Differential accumulation
b. Mergers
c. Political economy
d. Peace dividend

23.

The _________ was the first United States Federal statute to limit cartels and monopolies. It falls under antitrust law.

The Act provides: 'Every contract, combination in the form of trust or otherwise, or conspiracy, in restraint of trade or commerce among the several States, or with foreign nations, is declared to be illegal'. The Act also provides: 'Every person who shall monopolize, or attempt to monopolize, or combine or conspire with any other person or persons, to monopolize any part of the trade or commerce among the several States, or with foreign nations, shall be deemed guilty of a felony [. . . ]' The Act put responsibility upon government attorneys and district courts to pursue and investigate trusts, companies and organizations suspected of violating the Act. The Clayton Act extended the right to sue under the antitrust laws to 'any person who shall be injured in his business or property by reason of anything forbidden in the antitrust laws.' Under the Clayton Act, private parties may sue in U.S. district court and should they prevail, they may be awarded treble damages and the cost of suit, including reasonable attorney's fees.

a. 1921 recession
b. 130-30 fund
c. 100-year flood
d. Sherman Antitrust Act

24. A United States Treasury security is a government debt issued by the United States Department of the Treasury through the Bureau of the Public Debt. Treasury securities are the debt financing instruments of the United States Federal government, and they are often referred to simply as Treasuries. There are four types of marketable treasury securities: _________, Treasury notes, Treasury bonds, and Treasury Inflation Protected Securities (TIPS.)

a. Lawcards
b. Debt to Assets
c. Labour battalions
d. Treasury bills

25. The _________ consists of a number of economic theories which describe the nature of the firm, company including its existence, its behaviour, and its relationship with the market.

In simplified terms, the _________ aims to answer these questions:

1. Existence - why do firms emerge, why are not all transactions in the economy mediated over the market?
2. Boundaries - why the boundary between firms and the market is located exactly there? Which transactions are performed internally and which are negotiated on the market?
3. Organization - why are firms structured in such specific way? What is the interplay of formal and informal relationships?

Despite looking simple, these questions are not answered by the established economic theory, which usually views firms as given, and treats them as black boxes without any internal structure.

The First World War period saw a change of emphasis in economic theory away from industry-level analysis which mainly included analysing markets to analysis at the level of the firm, as it became increasingly clear that perfect competition was no longer an adequate model of how firms behaved. Economic theory till then had focussed on trying to understand markets alone and there had been little study on understanding why firms or organisations exist.

a. Policy Ineffectiveness Proposition
b. Khazzoom-Brookes postulate
c. Technology gap
d. Theory of the firm

26. _________ was a predominant American integrated oil producing, transporting, refining, and marketing company. Established in 1870 as an Ohio Corporation, it was the largest oil refiner in the world and operated as a major company trust and was one of the world's first and largest multinational corporations until it was broken up by the United States Supreme Court in 1911. John D. Rockefeller was a founder, chairman and major shareholder, and the company made him a billionaire and eventually the richest man in history.

a. Standard Oil
b. 100-year flood
c. 1921 recession
d. 130-30 fund

27. _________, known in the United States as antitrust law, has three main elements:

- prohibiting agreements or practices that restrict free trading and competition between business entities. This includes in particular the repression of cartels.
- banning abusive behaviour by a firm dominating a market, or anti-competitive practices that tend to lead to such a dominant position. Practices controlled in this way may include predatory pricing, tying, price gouging, refusal to deal, and many others.
- supervising the mergers and acquisitions of large corporations, including some joint ventures. Transactions that are considered to threaten the competitive process can be prohibited altogether, or approved subject to 'remedies' such as an obligation to divest part of the merged business or to offer licences or access to facilities to enable other businesses to continue competing.

The substance and practice of _________ varies from jurisdiction to jurisdiction. Protecting the interests of consumers (consumer welfare) and ensuring that entrepreneurs have an opportunity to compete in the market economy are often treated as important objectives. _________ is closely connected with law on deregulation of access to markets, state aids and subsidies, the privatisation of state owned assets and the establishment of independent sector regulators. In recent decades, _________ has been viewed as a way to provide better public services.

a. Competition law
b. Fee simple
c. Due diligence
d. Hostile work environment

28. The _________ is an independent agency of the United States government, established in 1914 by the _________ Act. Its principal mission is the promotion of 'consumer protection' and the elimination and prevention of what regulators perceive to be harmfully 'anti-competitive' business practices, such as coercive monopoly.

The _________ Act was one of President Wilson's major acts against trusts.

a. 130-30 fund
b. 100-year flood
c. 1921 recession
d. Federal Trade Commission

29. The _________ of 1914 (15 U.S.C Â§Â§ 41-58, as amended) established the Federal Trade Commission (FTC), a bipartisan body of five members appointed by the President of the United States for seven year terms. This Commission was authorized to issue Cease and Desist orders to large corporations to curb unfair trade practices. This Act also gave more flexibility to the US congress for judicial matters.

a. Buydown
b. Minimum wage law
c. Competition law theory
d. Federal Trade Commission Act

30. A _________ is a set of companies with interlocking business relationships and shareholdings. It is a type of business group.

The prototypical _________ are those which appeared in Japan during the 'economic miracle' following World War II.

a. 130-30 fund
b. Keiretsu
c. 1921 recession
d. 100-year flood

31. A _________ association is a financial institution that specializes in accepting savings deposits and making mortgage and other loans. The S'L or thrift term is mainly used in the United States; similar institutions in the United Kingdom, Ireland and some Commonwealth countries include building societies and trustee savings banks.

They are often mutually held, meaning that the depositors and borrowers are members with voting rights, and have the ability to direct the financial and managerial goals of the organization, similar to the policyholders of a mutual insurance company.

a. Participating policy
b. Fonds commun de placement
c. Collective investment scheme
d. Savings and Loan

32. A _________ is an agreement between businesses, usually motivated by cost reduction and improved service for the customer. Alliances are often bounded by a single agreement with equitable risk and opportunity share for all parties involved and are typically managed by an integrated project team. An example of this is code sharing in airline alliances.
a. Golden Boot Compensation
b. Market entry
c. Golden parachute
d. Business alliance

33. _________s is the social science that studies the production, distribution, and consumption of goods and services. The term _________s comes from the Ancient Greek oá¼°κονομÎ¯α from oá¼¶κος (oikos, 'house') + vÏŒμος (nomos, 'custom' or 'law'), hence 'rules of the house(hold)'. Current _________ models developed out of the broader field of political economy in the late 19th century, owing to a desire to use an empirical approach more akin to the physical sciences.
a. Energy economics
b. Economic
c. Inflation
d. Opportunity cost

34. The term _________ refers to government debt, expenditures and revenues, or to finance (particularly financial revenue) in general.

- _________ deficit is the budget deficit of federal or local government
- _________ policy is the discretionary spending of governments. Contrasts with monetary policy.
- _________ year and _________ quarter are reporting periods for firms and other agencies.

a. Procter ' Gamble
b. Bucket shop
c. Drawdown
d. Fiscal

35. In economics, _________ is the use of government spending and revenue collection to influence the economy.

_________ can be contrasted with the other main type of economic policy, monetary policy, which attempts to stabilize the economy by controlling interest rates and the supply of money. The two main instruments of _________ are government spending and taxation.

a. 100-year flood
b. Sustainable investment rule
c. Fiscal policy
d. Fiscalism

36. _________ is the process by which the government, central bank (ii) availability of money, and (iii) cost of money or rate of interest, in order to attain a set of objectives oriented towards the growth and stability of the economy. Monetary theory provides insight into how to craft optimal _________.

_________ is referred to as either being an expansionary policy where an expansionary policy increases the total supply of money in the economy, and a contractionary policy decreases the total money supply.

a. 100-year flood
b. 1921 recession
c. 130-30 fund
d. Monetary policy

37. To _________ is to impose a financial charge or other levy upon a taxpayer by a state or the functional equivalent of a state.

_________es are also imposed by many subnational entities. _________es consist of direct _________ or indirect _________, and may be paid in money or as its labour equivalent (often but not always unpaid.)

a. 100-year flood
b. 130-30 fund
c. 1921 recession
d. Tax

38. In economics, _________ is the total demand for final goods and services in the economy (Y) at a given time and price level. It is the amount of goods and services in the economy that will be purchased at all possible price levels. This is the demand for the gross domestic product of a country when inventory levels are static.

a. Aggregate expenditure
b. Aggregate supply
c. Aggregation problem
d. Aggregate demand

1. In economics, a _________ exists when the production or use of goods and services by the market is not efficient. That is, there exists another outcome where all involved can be made better off. _________s can be viewed as scenarios where individuals' pursuit of pure self-interest leads to results that are not efficient - that can be improved upon from the societal point-of-view.

a. Fixed exchange rate
b. General equilibrium
c. Financial economics
d. Market failure

2. In economics, _________ is the ability of a firm to alter the market price of a good or service. A firm with _________ can raise prices without losing all customers to competitors.

When a firm has _________ it faces a downward-sloping demand curve.

a. Pacman conjecture
b. Price makers
c. Market power
d. Revenue-cap regulation

3. _________ was a survey conducted by the U.S. Department of Justice to gauge the prevalence of alcohol and illegal drug use among prior arrestees. It was a reformulation of the prior Drug Use Forecasting (DUF) program, focused on five drugs in particular: cocaine, marijuana, methamphetamine, opiates, and PCP.

Participants were randomly selected from arrest records in major metropolitan areas; because no personally identifying information is taken from each record chosen, the resulting data can be correlated to arrest rates, but not to the total population of persons charged.

a. ACEA agreement
b. ACCRA Cost of Living Index
c. Arrestee Drug Abuse Monitoring
d. AD-IA Model

4. In economics, an externality or spillover of an economic transaction is an impact on a party that is not directly involved in the transaction. In such a case, prices do not reflect the full costs or benefits in production or consumption of a product or service. A positive impact is called an _________, while a negative impact is called an external cost.

a. External benefit
b. AD-IA Model
c. ACCRA Cost of Living Index
d. ACEA agreement

5. Many _________ are related to the environmental consequences of production and use

- Systemic risk describes the risks to the overall economy arising from the risks which the banking system takes. That the private costs of banking failure may be smaller than the social costs justifies banking regulations, although regulations could create a moral hazard.

- Anthropogenic climate change is attributed to greenhouse gas emissions from burning oil, gas, and coal. Global warming has been ranked as the #1 externality of all economic activity, in the magnitude of potential harms and yet remains unmitigated.

a. Green certificate
b. White certificates
c. Total Economic Value
d. Negative externalities

6. _________ was a Scottish moral philosopher and a pioneer of political economy. One of the key figures of the Scottish Enlightenment, Smith is the author of The Theory of Moral Sentiments and An Inquiry into the Nature and Causes of the Wealth of Nations. The latter, usually abbreviated as The Wealth of Nations, is considered his magnum opus and the first modern work of economics.

a. Adolph Fischer
b. Adam Smith
c. Alan Greenspan
d. Adolf Hitler

7. _________ is an economic system in which wealth, and the means of producing wealth, are privately owned. Through _________, the land, labor, and capital are owned, operated, and traded for the purpose of generating profits, without force or fraud, by private individuals either singly or jointly, and investments, distribution, income, production, pricing and supply of goods, commodities and services are determined by voluntary private decision in a market economy. A distinguishing feature of _________ is that each person owns his or her own labor and therefore is allowed to sell the use of it to employers.

a. Late capitalism
b. Capitalism
c. Socialism for the rich and capitalism for the poor
d. Creative capitalism

8. _________ is a practice of protecting the environment, on individual, organisational or governmental level, for the benefit of the natural environment and (or) humans.

Due to the pressures of population and technology the biophysical environment is being degraded, sometimes permanently. This has been recognised and governments began placing restraints on activities that caused environmental degradation.

a. ACEA agreement
b. AD-IA Model
c. Environmental protection
d. ACCRA Cost of Living Index

9. In economics _________ is defined as the sum of private and external costs. Economic theorists ascribe individual decision-making to a calculation costs and benefits. Rational choice theory assumes that individuals only consider their own private costs when making decisions, not the costs that may be borne by others.

a. Cost-Volume-Profit Analysis
b. Khozraschyot
c. Psychic cost
d. Social cost

10. _________s is the social science that studies the production, distribution, and consumption of goods and services. The term _________s comes from the Ancient Greek oá¼°κονομΐα from oá¼¶κος (oikos, 'house') + νΪŒμος (nomos, 'custom' or 'law'), hence 'rules of the house(hold)'. Current _________ models developed out of the broader field of political economy in the late 19th century, owing to a desire to use an empirical approach more akin to the physical sciences.

a. Energy economics
b. Economic
c. Inflation
d. Opportunity cost

11. _________ is the increase in the amount of the goods and services produced by an economy over time. It is conventionally measured as the percent rate of increase in real gross domestic product, or real GDP. Growth is usually calculated in real terms, i.e. inflation-adjusted terms, in order to net out the effect of inflation on the price of the goods and services produced.

a. Economic growth
b. ACCRA Cost of Living Index
c. AD-IA Model
d. ACEA agreement

12. _________ is used to assign the available resources in an economic way. It is part of resource management.

In strategic planning,is a plan for using available resources, for example human resources, especially in the near term, to achieve goals for the future.

a. 1921 recession
b. Resource allocation
c. 100-year flood
d. 130-30 fund

13. A _________ is the exclusive authority to determine how a resource is used, whether that resource is owned by government or by individuals. All economic goods have a _________s attribute. This attribute has three broad components

1. The right to use the good
2. The right to earn income from the good
3. The right to transfer the good to others

The concept of _________s as used by economists and legal scholars are related but distinct. The distinction is largely seen in the economists' focus on the ability of an individual or collective to control the use of the good.

a. Post-sale restraint
b. Holder in due course
c. High-reeve
d. Property right

14. _________, short for Ecological taxation, can refer to:

A policy that introduces taxes intended to promote ecologically sustainable activities via economic incentives. Such a policy can complement or avert the need for regulatory approaches. Often, such a policy intends to maintain overall tax revenue by proportionately reducing other taxes, e.g. on human labor and renewable resources, in which case it is known as the green tax shift towards ecological taxation.

a. AD-IA Model
b. ACEA agreement
c. Ecotax
d. ACCRA Cost of Living Index

15. To _________ is to impose a financial charge or other levy upon a taxpayer by a state or the functional equivalent of a state.

_________es are also imposed by many subnational entities. _________es consist of direct _________ or indirect _________, and may be paid in money or as its labour equivalent (often but not always unpaid.)

a. Tax
b. 130-30 fund
c. 100-year flood
d. 1921 recession

16. To tax is to impose a financial charge or other levy upon a taxpayer by a state or the functional equivalent of a state.

_________ are also imposed by many subnational entities. _________ consist of direct tax or indirect tax, and may be paid in money or as its labour equivalent (often but not always unpaid.)

a. 130-30 fund
b. Taxes
c. 100-year flood
d. 1921 recession

17. A _________ describes one of a number of pieces of legislation relating to the reduction of smog and air pollution in general. The use by governments to enforce clean air standards has contributed to an improvement in human health and longer life spans. Critics argue it has also sapped corporate profits and contributed to outsourcing, while defenders counter that improved environmental air quality has generated more jobs than it has eliminated.

a. 100-year flood
b. Clean Air Act
c. Smog
d. 130-30 fund

18. _________ is any long-term change in the patterns of average weather of a specific region or the Earth as a whole. _________ reflects abnormal variations to the Earth's climate and subsequent effects on other parts of the Earth, such as in the ice caps over durations ranging from decades to millions of years.

In recent usage, especially in the context of environmental policy, _________ usually refers to changes in modern climate

a. 1921 recession
b. 100-year flood
c. 130-30 fund
d. Climate Change

19. _________ is an administrative approach used to control pollution by providing economic incentives for achieving reductions in the emissions of pollutants. It is sometimes called cap and trade. A coal power plant in Germany.

a. Efficient energy use
b. ACCRA Cost of Living Index
c. International Climate Science Coalition
d. Emissions trading

20. An _________ or Å"conomic system is a system that involves the production, distribution and consumption of goods and services between the entities in a particular society. It is the method used by society to produce and distribute goods and services. The _________ is composed of people and institutions, including their relationships to productive resources, such as through the convention of property.

a. Intention economy
b. Indicative planning
c. Information economy
d. Economic system

21. _________ was an American economist, statistician and public intellectual, and a recipient of the Nobel Memorial Prize in Economic Sciences. He is best known among scholars for his theoretical and empirical research, especially consumption analysis, monetary history and theory, and for his demonstration of the complexity of stabilization policy. A global public followed his restatement of a political philosophy that insisted on minimizing the role of government in favor of the private sector.

a. Adam Smith
b. Milton Friedman
c. Adolph Fischer
d. Adolf Hitler

22. A _________ in general is a certificate of ownership that gold owners hold instead of storing the actual gold. It has both a historic meaning as a US paper currency (1882-1933) and a current meaning as a way to invest in gold. A picture of a _________ Series 1934 $100 _________, Obverse $100,000 _________, Obverse

The _________ was used from 1882 to 1933 in the United States as a form of paper currency.

a. 130-30 fund
b. 1921 recession
c. Gold certificate
d. 100-year flood

23. A _________ is an object whose consumption increases the utility of the consumer, for which the quantity demanded exceeds the quantity supplied at zero price. _________s are usually modeled as having diminishing marginal utility. The first individual purchase has high utility; the second has less.

a. Merit good
b. Composite good
c. Pie method
d. Good

24. A _________ is defined in economics as a good that exhibits these properties:

- Excludable - it is reasonably possible to prevent a class of consumers (e.g. those who have not paid for it) from consuming the good.
- Rivalrous - consumptions by one consumer prevents simultaneous consumption by other consumers. _________s satisfies an individual want while public good satisfies a collective want of the society.

A _________ is the opposite of a public good, as they are almost exclusively made for profit.

An example of the _________ is bread: bread eaten by a given person cannot be consumed by another (rivalry), and it is easy for a baker to refuse to trade a loaf (excludable

a. Positional goods
b. Demerit good
c. Pie method
d. Private good

25. _________ is an online peer-reviewed magazine published by the Agricultural ' Applied Economics Association (AAEA) for readers interested in the policy and management of agriculture, the food industry, natural resources, rural communities, and the environment. _________ is published quarterly and is available free online. It is currently one of three outreach products offered by AAEA, along with the more timely Policy Issues and the forthcoming Shared Materials section of the AAEA Web site.

a. 1921 recession
b. 100-year flood
c. 130-30 fund
d. Choices

26. In economics, a _________ is a good that is non-rivaled and non-excludable. This means, respectively, that consumption of the good by one individual does not reduce availability of the good for consumption by others; and that no one can be effectively excluded from using the good. In the real world, there may be no such thing as an absolutely non-rivaled and non-excludable good; but economists think that some goods approximate the concept closely enough for the analysis to be economically useful.

a. Public good
b. Demand-pull theory
c. Neoclassical synthesis
d. Happiness economics

27. _________ is the public sector analogy to market failure and occurs when a government intervention causes a more inefficient allocation of goods and resources than would occur without that intervention. Likewise, the government's failure to intervene in a market failure that would result in a socially preferable mix of output is referred to as passive _________ (Weimer and Vining, 2004.) Just as with market failures, there are many different kinds of _________s that describe corresponding distortions.

a. Privatizing profits and socializing losses
b. Natural monopoly
c. Government-granted monopoly
d. Government failure

28. _________ in economic theory is the use of modern economic tools to study problems that are traditionally in the province of political science.

In particular, it studies the behavior of politicians and government officials as mostly self-interested agents and their interactions in the social system either as such or under alternative constitutional rules. These can be represented a number of ways, including standard constrained utility maximization, game theory, or decision theory.

a. Public interest theory
b. Paradox of voting
c. Rational ignorance
d. Public choice

29. _________ is the trading of favors or quid pro quo, such as vote trading by legislative members to obtain passage of actions of interest to each legislative member. It is also the 'cross quoting' of papers by academics in order to drive up reference counts. The Nuttall Encyclopedia describes log-rolling as 'mutual praise by authors of each other's work.' American frontiersman Davy Crockett was one of the first to apply the term to legislation:

The first known use of the term was by Congressman Davy Crockett, who said on the floor (of the U.S. House of Representatives) in 1835, 'my people don't like me to log-roll in their business, and vote away pre-emption rights to fellows in other states that never kindle a fire on their own land.'

The widest accepted origin is the old custom of neighbors assisting each other with the moving of logs.

a. Logrolling
b. 100-year flood
c. 1921 recession
d. 130-30 fund

30. In economics, _________ is how a natione;s total economy is distributed among its population. ._________ has always been a central concern of economic theory and economic policy. Classical economists such as Adam Smith, Thomas Malthus and David Ricardo were mainly concerned with factor _________, that is, the distribution of income between the main factors of production, land, labour and capital.

a. Equipment trust certificate
b. Income distribution
c. Authorised capital
d. Eco commerce

31. _________ in political thought refers to economic theories of social organization advocating collective ownership and administration of the means of production and distribution of goods, and a society characterized by equality for all individuals, with an egalitarian method of compensation. Modern _________ originated in the late 19th-century intellectual and working class political movement that criticized the effects of industrialization and private ownership on society. Karl Marx posited that _________ would be achieved via class struggle and a proletarian revolution after a transitional stage from capitalism called the dictatorship of the proletariat.

a. Adolph Fischer
b. Socialism
c. Adolf Hitler
d. Adam Smith

32. _________ is the shortage of common things such as food, clothing, shelter and safe drinking water, all of which determine the quality of life. It may also include the lack of access to opportunities such as education and employment which aid the escape from _________ and/or allow one to enjoy the respect of fellow citizens. According to Mollie Orshansky who developed the _________ measurements used by the U.S. government, 'to be poor is to be deprived of those goods and services and pleasures which others around us take for granted.' Ongoing debates over causes, effects and best ways to measure _________, directly influence the design and implementation of _________-reduction programs and are therefore relevant to the fields of public administration and international development.

a. Poverty map
b. Poverty
c. Growth Elasticity of Poverty
d. Liberal welfare reforms

33. _________ is the United States of America's federal assistance program, formerly known as 'welfare'. It began on July 1, 1997, and succeeded the Aid to Families with Dependent Children program, providing cash assistance to indigent American families with dependent children through the United States Department of Health and Human Services. Prior to 1997, the federal government designed the overall program requirements and guidelines, while states administered the program and determined eligibility for benefits.

a. 130-30 fund
b. Temporary Assistance for Needy Families
c. 100-year flood
d. 1921 recession

34. _________ is a branch of economics that deals with the performance, structure, and behavior of a national or regional economy as a whole. Along with microeconomics, _________ is one of the two most general fields in economics. It is the study of the behavior and decision-making of entire economies.

a. Nominal value
b. New Trade Theory
c. Tobit model
d. Macroeconomics

1. The _________, a unit of the United States Department of Labor, is the principal fact-finding agency for the U.S. government in the broad field of labor economics and statistics. The BLS is an independent national statistical agency that collects, processes, analyzes, and disseminates essential statistical data to the American public, the U.S. Congress, other Federal agencies, State and local governments, business, and labor representatives. The BLS also serves as a statistical resource to the Department of Labor.

a. Gross world product
b. Gross Regional Product
c. Gross national product
d. Bureau of Labor Statistics

2. _________ is a broad label that refers to any individuals or households that use goods and services generated within the economy. The concept of a _________ is used in different contexts, so that the usage and significance of the term may vary.

Typically when business people and economists talk of _________s they are talking about person as _________, an aggregated commodity item with little individuality other than that expressed in the buy/not-buy decision.

a. Consumer
b. 1921 recession
c. 100-year flood
d. 130-30 fund

3. A _________ is a measure of the average price of consumer goods and services purchased by households. A _________ measures a price change for a constant market basket of goods and services from one period to the next within the same area (city, region, or nation.) It is a price index determined by measuring the price of a standard group of goods meant to represent the typical market basket of a typical urban consumer.

a. CPI
b. Cost-of-living index
c. Consumer Price Index
d. Lipstick index

4. _________s is the social science that studies the production, distribution, and consumption of goods and services. The term _________s comes from the Ancient Greek oá¼°κονομΐα from oá¼¶κος (oikos, 'house') + vÏŒμος (nomos, 'custom' or 'law'), hence 'rules of the house(hold)'. Current _________ models developed out of the broader field of political economy in the late 19th century, owing to a desire to use an empirical approach more akin to the physical sciences.

a. Opportunity cost
b. Inflation
c. Energy economics
d. Economic

5. An _________ is a statistic about the economy. _________s allow analysis of economic performance and predictions of future performance.

_________s include various indices, earnings reports, and economic summaries, such as unemployment, housing starts, Consumer Price Index (a measure for inflation), industrial production, bankruptcies, Gross Domestic Product, broadband internet penetration, retail sales, stock market prices, and money supply changes.

a. Economic Vulnerability Index
b. Internationalization Index
c. Economic indicator
d. ACCRA Cost of Living Index

6. _________ in economics and business is the result of an exchange and from that trade we assign a numerical monetary value to a good, service or asset. If Alice trades Bob 4 apples for an orange, the _________ of an orange is 4 apples. Inversely, the _________ of an apple is 1/4 oranges.

a. Price book
b. Price war
c. Premium pricing
d. Price

7. A _________ is a normalized average (typically a weighted average) of prices for a given class of goods or services in a given region, during a given interval of time. It is a statistic designed to help to compare how these prices, taken as a whole, differ between time periods or geographical locations.

Price indices have several potential uses.

a. Product sabotage
b. Two-part tariff
c. Transactional Net Margin Method
d. Price Index

8. Unemployment occurs when a person is available to work and seeking work but currently without work. The prevalence of unemployment is usually measured using the _________, which is defined as the percentage of those in the labor force who are unemployed. The _________ is also used in economic studies and economic indexes such as the United States' Conference Board's Index of Leading Indicators as a measure of the state of the macroeconomics.

a. ACCRA Cost of Living Index
b. Unemployment rate
c. AD-IA Model
d. ACEA agreement

9. The Organization for Economic Co-operation and Development defines the _________ as the percentage of the working age population (ages 15 to 64 in most OECD countries) who are currently employed. According to the International Labour Organization, a person is considered employed if they have worked at least 1 hour in 'gainful' employment.

a. Employment rate
b. Informational interview
c. Underemployment
d. Encore career

10. In economics, the people in the _________ are the suppliers of labor. The _________ is all the nonmilitary people who are employed or unemployed. In 2005, the worldwide _________ was over 3 billion people.

a. Grenelle agreements
b. Departmentalization
c. Distributed workforce
d. Labor force

11. The term _________ refers to economy-wide fluctuations in production or economic activity over several months or years. These fluctuations occur around a long-term growth trend, and typically involve shifts over time between periods of relatively rapid economic growth (expansion or boom), and periods of relative stagnation or decline (contraction or recession.)

These fluctuations are often measured using the growth rate of real gross domestic product.

a. Tobit model
b. Consumer theory
c. Nominal value
d. Business cycle

12. Economists distinguish between various types of unemployment, including _________, frictional unemployment, structural unemployment and classical unemployment. Some additional types of unemployment that are occasionally mentioned are seasonal unemployment, hardcore unemployment, and hidden unemployment. Real-world unemployment may combine different types.

a. Structural unemployment
b. Types of unemployment
c. Seasonal unemployment
d. Cyclical unemployment

13. Economists distinguish between various types of unemployment, including cyclical unemployment, _________, structural unemployment and classical unemployment. Some additional types of unemployment that are occasionally mentioned are seasonal unemployment, hardcore unemployment, and hidden unemployment. Real-world unemployment may combine different types.

a. Seasonal unemployment
b. Frictional unemployment
c. Types of unemployment
d. Structural unemployment

14. _________ is long-term and chronic unemployment arising from imbalances between the skills and other characteristics of workers in the market and the needs of employers. It involves a mismatch between workers looking for jobs and the vacancies available often despite the number of vacancies being similar to the number of unemployed people. In this case, the unemployed workers lack the specific skills required for the jobs, or are located in a different geographical region to the vacant jobs.

a. Frictional unemployment
b. Seasonal unemployment
c. Structural unemployment
d. Types of unemployment

15. The _________ is a concept of economic activity developed in particular by Milton Friedman and Edmund Phelps in the 1960s, both recipients of the Nobel prize in economics. In both cases, the development of the concept is cited as a main motivation behind the prize. It represents the hypothetical unemployment rate consistent with aggregate production being at the 'long-run' level.

a. Robertson lag
b. Romer Model
c. Real Business Cycle Theory
d. Natural rate of unemployment

16. In economics, _________ is a rise in the general level of prices of goods and services in an economy over a period of time. When the general price level rises, each unit of currency buys fewer goods and services; consequently, _________ is also a decline in the real value of money--a loss of purchasing power in the medium of exchange which is also the monetary unit of account in the economy. A chief measure of general price-level _________ is the general _________ rate, which is the percentage change in a general price index (normally the Consumer Price Index) over time.

a. Economic
b. Energy economics
c. Opportunity cost
d. Inflation

17. _________ is one of the four Ps of the marketing mix. The other three aspects are product, promotion, and place. It is also a key variable in microeconomic price allocation theory.

a. Premium pricing
b. Pricing
c. Guaranteed Maximum Price
d. Point of total assumption

18. A _________ is a situation that involves losing one quality or aspect of something in return for gaining another quality or aspect. It implies a decision to be made with full comprehension of both the upside and downside of a particular choice.

In economics the term is expressed as opportunity cost, referring the most preferred alternative given up.

a. Whitemail
b. Trade-off
c. Nonmarket
d. Friedman-Savage utility function

19. In statistics, a _________ is a value that allows data to be measured over time in terms of some base period ussually through a price index in order to distinguish between changes in the money value of GNP which result from a change in prices and those which result from a change in physical output. It is the measure of the price level for some quantity. A _________ serves as a price index in which the effects of inflation are nulled.

a. Market microstructure
b. Contingent employment
c. Blanket order
d. Deflator

20. A _________ measures average changes in prices received by domestic producers for their output. It is one of several price indices

Its importance is being undermined by the steady decline in manufactured goods as a share of spending.

A number of countries that now report a _________ previously reported a Wholesale Price Index.

a. Gross national product
b. Visible balance
c. Hemline index
d. Producer Price Index

21. _________ is the income of individuals or nations after adjusting for inflation. It is calculated by subtracting inflation from the nominal income. Real variables, such as _________, real GDP, and real interest rate are variables that are measured in physical units, while nominal variables such as nominal income, nominal GDP, and nominal interest rate are measured in monetary units.

a. Family income
b. Net national income
c. Windfall gain
d. Real income

22. Economics:

- _________,the desire to own something and the ability to pay for it
- _________ curve,a graphic representation of a _________ schedule
- _________ deposit, the money in checking accounts
- _________ pull theory,the theory that inflation occurs when _________ for goods and services exceeds existing supplies
- _________ schedule,a table that lists the quantity of a good a person will buy it each different price
- _________ side economics,the school of economics at believes government spending and tax cuts open economy by raising _________

.

a. McKesson ' Robbins scandal
b. Variability
c. Production
d. Demand

23. In algebra, a _________ is a function depending on n that associates a scalar, det(A), to an n×n square matrix A. The fundamental geometric meaning of a _________ is a scale factor for measure when A is regarded as a linear transformation. _________s are important both in calculus, where they enter the substitution rule for several variables, and in multilinear algebra.

For a fixed nonnegative integer n, there is a unique _________ function for the n×n matrices over any commutative ring R. In particular, this function exists when R is the field of real or complex numbers.

a. 1921 recession
b. 130-30 fund
c. Determinant
d. 100-year flood

24. _________ in political thought refers to economic theories of social organization advocating collective ownership and administration of the means of production and distribution of goods, and a society characterized by equality for all individuals, with an egalitarian method of compensation. Modern _________ originated in the late 19th-century intellectual and working class political movement that criticized the effects of industrialization and private ownership on society. Karl Marx posited that _________ would be achieved via class struggle and a proletarian revolution after a transitional stage from capitalism called the dictatorship of the proletariat.

a. Socialism
b. Adam Smith
c. Adolph Fischer
d. Adolf Hitler

25. In economics, a _________ is a graph of the costs of production as a function of total quantity produced. In a free market economy, productively efficient firms use these curves to find the optimal point of production, where they make the most profits. There are a few different types of _________s, each relevant to a different area of economics.

a. Phillips curve
b. Demand curve
c. Kuznets curve
d. Cost curve

26. In economics a _________ is an entity that owes a debt to someone else. The entity may be an individual, a firm, a government, a company or other legal person. The counterparty is called a creditor.

a. Senior stretch loan
b. Duration gap
c. Decision process tool
d. Debtor

27. _________ is a common market structure where many competing producers sell products that are differentiated from one another (ie. the products are substitutes, but are not exactly alike.) Many markets are monopolistically competitive, common examples include the markets for restaurants, cereal, clothing, shoes and service industries in large cities.

a. Perfect competition
b. Mathematical economics
c. Financial crisis
d. Monopolistic competition

28. In economics, _________ is the ratio of the percent change in one variable to the percent change in another variable. It is a tool for measuring the responsiveness of a function to changes in parameters in a relative way. Commonly analyzed are _________ of substitution, price and wealth.

a. Elasticity of demand
b. ACEA agreement
c. ACCRA Cost of Living Index
d. Elasticity

29. Price _________ is defined as the measure of responsiveness in the quantity demanded for a commodity as a result of change in price of the same commodity. It is a measure of how consumers react to a change in price. In other words, it is percentage change in quantity demanded by the percentage change in price of the same commodity.

a. ACCRA Cost of Living Index
b. ACEA agreement
c. Elasticity of demand
d. Elasticity

30. In economics, the _________ is a measure of inflation, the rate of increase of a price index (for example, a consumer price index.)It is the percentage rate of change in price level over time. The rate of decrease in the purchasing power of money is approximately equal.

It's used to calculate the real interest rate, as well as real increases in wages, and official measurements of this rate act as input variables to COLA adjustments and Inflation derivatives prices.

a. Equity value
b. Edgeworth paradox
c. Interest rate option
d. Inflation rate

31. A _________ is the price of a representative basket of wholesale goods. Some countries (like India and The Philippines) use _________ changes as a central measure of inflation. However, India and the United States now report a producer price index instead.

a. TED spread
b. Wholesale Price Index
c. Lagging indicator
d. Producer Price Index

32. In economics _________s are goods that are ultimately consumed rather than used in the production of another good. For example, a car sold to a consumer is a _________; the components such as tires sold to the car manufacturer are not; they are intermediate goods used to make the _________.

When used in measures of national income and output the term _________s only includes new goods.

a. Luxury good
b. Goods and services
c. Final good
d. Substitute good

33. A _________ in general is a certificate of ownership that gold owners hold instead of storing the actual gold. It has both a historic meaning as a US paper currency (1882-1933) and a current meaning as a way to invest in gold. A picture of a _________ Series 1934 $100 _________, Obverse $100,000 _________, Obverse

The _________ was used from 1882 to 1933 in the United States as a form of paper currency.

a. 130-30 fund
b. 1921 recession
c. 100-year flood
d. Gold certificate

34. A _________ is an object whose consumption increases the utility of the consumer, for which the quantity demanded exceeds the quantity supplied at zero price. _________s are usually modeled as having diminishing marginal utility. The first individual purchase has high utility; the second has less.

a. Merit good
b. Pie method
c. Good
d. Composite good

35. The _________ or gross domestic income (GDI), a basic measure of an economy's economic performance, is the market value of all final goods and services produced within the borders of a nation in a year. _________ can be defined in three ways, all of which are conceptually identical. First, it is equal to the total expenditures for all final goods and services produced within the country in a stipulated period of time (usually a 365-day year.)

a. Market structure
b. Monopolistic competition
c. Countercyclical
d. Gross domestic product

36. _________ is a fee paid on borrowed assets. It is the price paid for the use of borrowed money , or, money earned by deposited funds . Assets that are sometimes lent with _________ include money, shares, consumer goods through hire purchase, major assets such as aircraft, and even entire factories in finance lease arrangements.

a. Internal debt
b. Asset protection
c. Insolvency
d. Interest

37. An _________ is the price a borrower pays for the use of money they do not own, for instance a small company might borrow from a bank to kick start their business, and the return a lender receives for deferring the use of funds, by lending it to the borrower. _________s are normally expressed as a percentage rate over the period of one year.

_________s targets are also a vital tool of monetary policy and are used to control variables like investment, inflation, and unemployment.

a. Interest rate
b. Enterprise value
c. ACCRA Cost of Living Index
d. Arrow-Debreu model

38. _________ or producer goods are goods used as inputs in the production of other goods, such as partly finished goods. They are goods used in production of final goods. A firm may make then use _________, or make then sell, or buy then use them.

a. Intermediate goods
b. Income distribution
c. Economic forecasting
d. Inflation adjustment

39. In economics, _________ is the total demand for final goods and services in the economy (Y) at a given time and price level. It is the amount of goods and services in the economy that will be purchased at all possible price levels. This is the demand for the gross domestic product of a country when inventory levels are static.

a. Aggregate demand
b. Aggregate supply
c. Aggregation problem
d. Aggregate expenditure

40. _________ is an online peer-reviewed magazine published by the Agricultural ' Applied Economics Association (AAEA) for readers interested in the policy and management of agriculture, the food industry, natural resources, rural communities, and the environment. _________ is published quarterly and is available free online. It is currently one of three outreach products offered by AAEA, along with the more timely Policy Issues and the forthcoming Shared Materials section of the AAEA Web site.

a. 100-year flood
b. 130-30 fund
c. 1921 recession
d. Choices

41. In economics, the term _________ of income or _________ refers to a simple economic model which describes the reciprocal circulation of income between producers and consumers. In the _________ model, the inter-dependent entities of producer and consumer are referred to as 'firms' and 'households' respectively and provide each other with factors in order to facilitate the flow of income. Firms provide consumers with goods and services in exchange for consumer expenditure and 'factors of production' from households.

a. 130-30 fund
b. 1921 recession
c. Circular flow
d. 100-year flood

42. In economics, the _________ can be defined as the graph depicting the relationship between the price of a certain commodity, and the amount of it that consumers are willing and able to purchase at that given price. It is a graphic representation of a demand schedule. The _________ for all consumers together follows from the _________ of every individual consumer: the individual demands at each price are added together.

a. Kuznets curve
b. Wage curve
c. Cost curve
d. Demand curve

43. The _________ is one of three major groups of methodologies, called valuation approaches, used by appraisers. It is particularly common in commercial real estate appraisal and in business appraisal. The fundamental math is similar to the methods used for financial valuation, securities analysis, or bond pricing.

a. Income approach
b. ACEA agreement
c. Urban growth boundary
d. ACCRA Cost of Living Index

44. _________ is a macroeconomic measure of the size of an economy adjusted for price changes and inflation. It measures in constant prices the output of final goods and services and incomes within an economy. The formula for its definition is [(Nominal GDP)/(GDP deflator)] x 100, however, it is not calculated in this way.

a. Bureau of Labor Statistics
b. TED spread
c. Gross world product
d. Real gross domestic product

1. In economics, _________ is the total demand for final goods and services in the economy (Y) at a given time and price level. It is the amount of goods and services in the economy that will be purchased at all possible price levels. This is the demand for the gross domestic product of a country when inventory levels are static.

a. Aggregation problem
b. Aggregate supply
c. Aggregate expenditure
d. Aggregate demand

2. In economics, _________ is the total supply of goods and services produced by a national economy during a specific time period. It is the total amount of goods and services in the economy available at all possible price levels.

a. Aggregation problem
b. Aggregate expenditure
c. Aggregate demand
d. Aggregate supply

3. Economics:

- _________,the desire to own something and the ability to pay for it
- _________ curve,a graphic representation of a _________ schedule
- _________ deposit, the money in checking accounts
- _________ pull theory,the theory that inflation occurs when _________ for goods and services exceeds existing supplies
- _________ schedule,a table that lists the quantity of a good a person will buy it each different price
- _________ side economics,the school of economics at believes government spending and tax cuts open economy by raising _________

.

a. Production
b. Demand
c. McKesson ' Robbins scandal
d. Variability

4. In economics, the _________ can be defined as the graph depicting the relationship between the price of a certain commodity, and the amount of it that consumers are willing and able to purchase at that given price. It is a graphic representation of a demand schedule. The _________ for all consumers together follows from the _________ of every individual consumer: the individual demands at each price are added together.

a. Cost curve
b. Kuznets curve
c. Wage curve
d. Demand curve

5. _________ is a fee paid on borrowed assets. It is the price paid for the use of borrowed money , or, money earned by deposited funds . Assets that are sometimes lent with _________ include money, shares, consumer goods through hire purchase, major assets such as aircraft, and even entire factories in finance lease arrangements.

a. Internal debt
b. Interest
c. Insolvency
d. Asset protection

6. An _________ is the price a borrower pays for the use of money they do not own, for instance a small company might borrow from a bank to kick start their business, and the return a lender receives for deferring the use of funds, by lending it to the borrower. _________s are normally expressed as a percentage rate over the period of one year.

_________s targets are also a vital tool of monetary policy and are used to control variables like investment, inflation, and unemployment.

a. Arrow-Debreu model
b. Enterprise value
c. Interest rate
d. ACCRA Cost of Living Index

7. In economics, an _________ is any good or commodity, transported from one country to another country in a legitimate fashion, typically for use in trade. _________ goods or services are provided to foreign consumers by domestic producers. _________ is an important part of international trade.

a. AD-IA Model
b. ACCRA Cost of Living Index
c. ACEA agreement
d. Export

8. In economics, an _________ is any good (e.g. a commodity) or service brought into one country from another country in a legitimate fashion, typically for use in trade.It is a good that is brought in from another country for sale. _________ goods or services are provided to domestic consumers by foreign producers. An _________ in the receiving country is an export to the sending country.

a. Incoterms
b. Import quota
c. Economic integration
d. Import

9. _________ is exchange of capital, goods, and services across international borders or territories. In most countries, it represents a significant share of gross domestic product (GDP.) While _________ has been present throughout much of history , its economic, social, and political importance has been on the rise in recent centuries.

a. Import license
b. Intra-industry trade
c. International trade
d. Incoterms

10. The _________ is 'the basic residential unit in which economic production, consumption, inheritance, child rearing, and shelter are organized and carried out'; [the _________] 'may or may not be synonomous with family'.

The _________ is the basic unit of analysis in many social, microeconomic and government models. The term refers to all individuals who live in the same dwelling.

a. 130-30 fund
b. 100-year flood
c. Family economics
d. Household

11. _________s is the social science that studies the production, distribution, and consumption of goods and services. The term _________s comes from the Ancient Greek oá¼°κονομί̂α from oá¼¶κος (oikos, 'house') + vÏŒμος (nomos, 'custom' or 'law'), hence 'rules of the house(hold)'. Current _________ models developed out of the broader field of political economy in the late 19th century, owing to a desire to use an empirical approach more akin to the physical sciences.

a. Opportunity cost
b. Energy economics
c. Inflation
d. Economic

12. The term _________ refers to government debt, expenditures and revenues, or to finance (particularly financial revenue) in general.

- _________ deficit is the budget deficit of federal or local government
- _________ policy is the discretionary spending of governments. Contrasts with monetary policy.
- _________ year and _________ quarter are reporting periods for firms and other agencies.

.

a. Bucket shop
b. Drawdown
c. Fiscal
d. Procter ' Gamble

13. In economics, _________ is the use of government spending and revenue collection to influence the economy.

_________ can be contrasted with the other main type of economic policy, monetary policy, which attempts to stabilize the economy by controlling interest rates and the supply of money. The two main instruments of _________ are government spending and taxation.

a. Fiscal policy
b. Sustainable investment rule
c. 100-year flood
d. Fiscalism

14. _________ is the application of economic techniques to real estate markets. It tries to describe, explain, and predict patterns of prices, supply, and demand. The closely related fields of housing economics is narrower in scope, concentrating on residential real estate markets as does the research of real estate trends focus on the business and structural changes impacting the industry.

a. 100-year flood
b. 1921 recession
c. 130-30 fund
d. Real estate economics

15. _________ is the process by which the government, central bank (ii) availability of money, and (iii) cost of money or rate of interest, in order to attain a set of objectives oriented towards the growth and stability of the economy. Monetary theory provides insight into how to craft optimal _________.

_________ is referred to as either being an expansionary policy where an expansionary policy increases the total supply of money in the economy, and a contractionary policy decreases the total money supply.

a. 100-year flood
b. 130-30 fund
c. 1921 recession
d. Monetary policy

16. To _________ is to impose a financial charge or other levy upon a taxpayer by a state or the functional equivalent of a state.

_________es are also imposed by many subnational entities. _________es consist of direct _________ or indirect _________, and may be paid in money or as its labour equivalent (often but not always unpaid.)

a. 1921 recession
b. 130-30 fund
c. 100-year flood
d. Tax

17. Discounting is a financial mechanism in which a debtor obtains the right to delay payments to a creditor, for a defined period of time, in exchange for a charge or fee. Essentially, the party that owes money in the present purchases the right to delay the payment until some future date. The _________, or charge, is simply the difference between the original amount owed in the present and the amount that has to be paid in the future to settle the debt.

a. Certified Risk Manager
b. Reliability theory
c. Reinsurance
d. Discount

18. The _________ is an interest rate a central bank charges depository institutions that borrow reserves from it.

The term _________ has two meanings:

- the same as interest rate; the term 'discount' does not refer to the meaning of the word, but to the purpose of using the quantity, such as computations of present value, e.g. net present value or discounted cash flow

- the annual effective _________, which is the annual interest divided by the capital including that interest; this rate is lower than the interest rate; it corresponds to using the value after a year as the nominal value, and seeing the initial value as the nominal value minus a discount; it is used for Treasury Bills and similar financial instruments

The annual effective _________ is the annual interest divided by the capital including that interest, which is the interest rate divided by 100% plus the interest rate. It is the annual discount factor to be applied to the future cash flow, to find the discount, subtracted from a future value to find the value one year earlier.

For example, suppose there is a government bond that sells for $95 and pays $100 in a year's time.

a. Perpetuity
b. Discount rate
c. Stochastic volatility
d. Johansen test

19. _________ in economics and business is the result of an exchange and from that trade we assign a numerical monetary value to a good, service or asset. If Alice trades Bob 4 apples for an orange, the _________ of an orange is 4 apples. Inversely, the _________ of an apple is 1/4 oranges.

a. Premium pricing
b. Price book
c. Price war
d. Price

20. In algebra, a _________ is a function depending on n that associates a scalar, det(A), to an n×n square matrix A. The fundamental geometric meaning of a _________ is a scale factor for measure when A is regarded as a linear transformation. _________s are important both in calculus, where they enter the substitution rule for several variables, and in multilinear algebra.

For a fixed nonnegative integer n, there is a unique _________ function for the n×n matrices over any commutative ring R. In particular, this function exists when R is the field of real or complex numbers.

a. 130-30 fund
b. 100-year flood
c. Determinant
d. 1921 recession

21. In economic models, the _________ time frame assumes no fixed factors of production. Firms can enter or leave the marketplace, and the cost (and availability) of land, labor, raw materials, and capital goods can be assumed to vary. In contrast, in the short-run time frame, certain factors are assumed to be fixed, because there is not sufficient time for them to change.

a. Diseconomies of scale
b. Price/performance ratio
c. Productivity world
d. Long-run

22. _________ in economics refers to metrics and measures of output from production processes, per unit of input. Labor _________, for example, is typically measured as a ratio of output per labor-hour, an input. _________ may be conceived of as a metrics of the technical or engineering efficiency of production.

a. Piece work
b. Fordism
c. Production-possibility frontier
d. Productivity

23. Competition law, known in the United States as _________ law, has three main elements:

- prohibiting agreements or practices that restrict free trading and competition between business entities. This includes in particular the repression of cartels.
- banning abusive behaviour by a firm dominating a market, or anti-competitive practices that tend to lead to such a dominant position. Practices controlled in this way may include predatory pricing, tying, price gouging, refusal to deal, and many others.
- supervising the mergers and acquisitions of large corporations, including some joint ventures. Transactions that are considered to threaten the competitive process can be prohibited altogether, or approved subject to 'remedies' such as an obligation to divest part of the merged business or to offer licences or access to facilities to enable other businesses to continue competing.

The substance and practice of competition law varies from jurisdiction to jurisdiction. Protecting the interests of consumers (consumer welfare) and ensuring that entrepreneurs have an opportunity to compete in the market economy are often treated as important objectives. Competition law is closely connected with law on deregulation of access to markets, state aids and subsidies, the privatisation of state owned assets and the establishment of independent sector regulators. In recent decades, competition law has been viewed as a way to provide better public services.

a. Intellectual property law
b. United Kingdom competition law
c. Antitrust
d. Anti-Inflation Act

24. The _________ or gross domestic income (GDI), a basic measure of an economy's economic performance, is the market value of all final goods and services produced within the borders of a nation in a year. _________ can be defined in three ways, all of which are conceptually identical. First, it is equal to the total expenditures for all final goods and services produced within the country in a stipulated period of time (usually a 365-day year.)

a. Monopolistic competition
b. Gross domestic product
c. Market structure
d. Countercyclical

25. The supply of labor is the number of total hours that workers wish to work at a given real wage rate.

_________ curves are derived from the 'labor-leisure' trade-off. More hours worked earn higher incomes but necessitate a cut in the amount of leisure that workers enjoy.

a. Late capitalism
b. Creative capitalism
c. Human trafficking
d. Labor supply

26. _________ refers to the state of not requiring any outside aid, support for survival; it is therefore a type of personal or collective autonomy. On a large scale, a totally self-sufficient economy that does not trade with the outside world is called an autarky.

The term _________ is usually applied to varieties of sustainable living in which nothing is consumed outside of what is produced by the self-sufficient individuals.

a. Sustainability science
b. Sustainable forest management
c. Global Reporting Initiative
d. Self-sufficiency

27. _________ is a macroeconomic measure of the size of an economy adjusted for price changes and inflation. It measures in constant prices the output of final goods and services and incomes within an economy. The formula for its definition is [(Nominal GDP)/(GDP deflator)] x 100, however, it is not calculated in this way.

a. Gross world product
b. Bureau of Labor Statistics
c. Real Gross domestic product
d. TED spread

28. _________ is a broad label that refers to any individuals or households that use goods and services generated within the economy. The concept of a _________ is used in different contexts, so that the usage and significance of the term may vary.

Typically when business people and economists talk of _________s they are talking about person as _________, an aggregated commodity item with little individuality other than that expressed in the buy/not-buy decision.

a. 130-30 fund
b. 1921 recession
c. Consumer
d. 100-year flood

29. A _________ is a measure of the average price of consumer goods and services purchased by households. A _________ measures a price change for a constant market basket of goods and services from one period to the next within the same area (city, region, or nation.) It is a price index determined by measuring the price of a standard group of goods meant to represent the typical market basket of a typical urban consumer.

a. CPI
b. Cost-of-living index
c. Lipstick index
d. Consumer Price Index

30. _________ arises when aggregate demand in an economy outpaces aggregate supply. It involves inflation rising as real gross domestic product rises and unemployment falls, as the economy moves along the Phillips curve. This is commonly described as 'too much money chasing too few goods'.

a. Kinked demand curve
b. Marshallian demand function
c. Kinked demand
d. Demand-pull inflation

31. A _________ is a normalized average (typically a weighted average) of prices for a given class of goods or services in a given region, during a given interval of time. It is a statistic designed to help to compare how these prices, taken as a whole, differ between time periods or geographical locations.

Price indices have several potential uses.

a. Two-part tariff
b. Product sabotage
c. Transactional Net Margin Method
d. Price Index

32. A _________ is an event that suddenly changes the price of a commodity or service. It may be caused by a sudden increase or decrease in the supply of a particular good. This sudden change affects the equilibrium price.

a. Supply shock
b. SIMIC
c. Friedman rule
d. Demand shock

33. In economics, _________ is a rise in the general level of prices of goods and services in an economy over a period of time. When the general price level rises, each unit of currency buys fewer goods and services; consequently, _________ is also a decline in the real value of money--a loss of purchasing power in the medium of exchange which is also the monetary unit of account in the economy. A chief measure of general price-level _________ is the general _________ rate, which is the percentage change in a general price index (normally the Consumer Price Index) over time.

a. Economic
b. Energy economics
c. Opportunity cost
d. Inflation

34. _________ is a type of inflation caused by substantial increases in the cost of important goods or services where no suitable alternative is available. A situation that has been often cited of this was the oil crisis of the 1970s, which some economists see as a major cause of the inflation experienced in the Western world in that decade. It is argued that this inflation resulted from increases in the cost of petroleum imposed by the member states of OPEC.

a. Cost-push inflation
b. Chronic inflation
c. Headline inflation
d. Mundell-Tobin effect

35. _________ is an economic situation in which inflation and economic stagnation occur simultaneously and remain unchecked for a period of time. The portmanteau _________ is generally attributed to British politician Iain Macleod, who coined the term in a speech to Parliament in 1965. The concept is notable partly because, in postwar macroeconomic theory, inflation and recession were regarded as mutually exclusive, and also because _________ has generally proven to be difficult and costly to eradicate once it gets started.

a. Chronic inflation
b. Stagflation
c. Real interest rate
d. Price/wage spiral

36. The term _________ refers to economy-wide fluctuations in production or economic activity over several months or years. These fluctuations occur around a long-term growth trend, and typically involve shifts over time between periods of relatively rapid economic growth (expansion or boom), and periods of relative stagnation or decline (contraction or recession.)

These fluctuations are often measured using the growth rate of real gross domestic product.

a. Business cycle
b. Tobit model
c. Nominal value
d. Consumer theory

37. In economics, a _________ is a sudden event that increases or decreases demand for goods or services temporarily. A positive _________ increases demand and a negative _________ decreases demand. Prices of goods and services are affected in both cases.

a. Demand shock
b. Lucas-Islands model
c. Robertson lag
d. War economy

38. _________ and Keynesian Theory) is a macroeconomic theory based on the ideas of 20th-century British economist John Maynard Keynes. _________ argues that private sector decisions sometimes lead to inefficient macroeconomic outcomes and therefore advocates active policy responses by the public sector, including monetary policy actions by the central bank and fiscal policy actions by the government to stabilize output over the business cycle.

The theories forming the basis of _________ were first presented in The General Theory of Employment, Interest and Money, published in 1936.

a. Market failure
b. Deflation
c. Rational choice theory
d. Keynesian economics

39. In economics, a _________ is a general slowdown in economic activity over a sustained period of time, or a business cycle contraction. During _________s, many macroeconomic indicators vary in a similar way. Production as measured by Gross Domestic Product (GDP), employment, investment spending, capacity utilization, household incomes and business profits all fall during _________s.

a. Treasury View
b. Leading indicators
c. Monetary economics
d. Recession

40. The term _________s refers to wages that have been adjusted for inflation. This term is used in contrast to nominal wages or unadjusted wages.

The use of adjusted figures is in undertaking some form of economic analysis.

a. Living wage
b. Profit sharing
c. Federal Wage System
d. Real wage

1. The term _________ refers to government debt, expenditures and revenues, or to finance (particularly financial revenue) in general.

- _________ deficit is the budget deficit of federal or local government
- _________ policy is the discretionary spending of governments. Contrasts with monetary policy.
- _________ year and _________ quarter are reporting periods for firms and other agencies.

.

a. Drawdown
b. Bucket shop
c. Fiscal
d. Procter ' Gamble

2. A _________ is a period used for calculating annual financial statements in businesses and other organizations. In many jurisdictions, regulatory laws regarding accounting and taxation require such reports once per twelve months, but do not require that the period reported on constitutes a calendar year (i.e., January through December.) _________s vary between businesses and countries.

a. 130-30 fund
b. 1921 recession
c. 100-year flood
d. Fiscal year

3. A _________ occurs when an entity spends more money than it takes in. The opposite of a _________ is a budget surplus. Debt is essentially an accumulated flow of deficits.

a. Lump-sum tax
b. Funding body
c. Public Financial Management
d. Budget deficit

4. To _________ is to impose a financial charge or other levy upon a taxpayer by a state or the functional equivalent of a state.

_________es are also imposed by many subnational entities. _________es consist of direct _________ or indirect _________, and may be paid in money or as its labour equivalent (often but not always unpaid.)

a. 1921 recession
b. 100-year flood
c. 130-30 fund
d. Tax

5. To tax is to impose a financial charge or other levy upon a taxpayer by a state or the functional equivalent of a state.

_________ are also imposed by many subnational entities. _________ consist of direct tax or indirect tax, and may be paid in money or as its labour equivalent (often but not always unpaid.)

a. 1921 recession
b. 100-year flood
c. 130-30 fund
d. Taxes

6. In economics, a _________ is a redistribution of income in the market system. These payments are considered to be nonexhaustive because they do not directly absorb resources or create output. Examples of certain _________s include welfare (financial aid), social security, and government subsidies for certain businesses (firms.)

a. 1921 recession
b. 130-30 fund
c. 100-year flood
d. Transfer payment

7. A _________ is the transfer of wealth from one party (such as a person or company) to another. A _________ is usually made in exchange for the provision of goods, services or both, or to fulfill a legal obligation.

The simplest and oldest form of _________ is barter, the exchange of one good or service for another.

a. Payment
b. Soft count
c. Social gravity
d. Going concern

8. _________ are the income that is gained by governments because of taxation of the people.

Just as there are different types of tax, the form in which _________ is collected also differs; furthermore, the agency that collects the tax may not be part of central government, but may be an alternative third-party licenced to collect tax which they themselves will use. For example:

- In the UK, the DVLA collects road tax, which is then passed on the treasury.

_________s on purchases can come from two forms: 'tax' itself is a percentage of the price added to the purchase (such as sales tax in US states, or VAT in the UK), while 'duty' is a fixed amount added to the purchase price (such as is commonly found on cigarettes.) In order to calculate the total tax raised from these sales, we must work out the effective tax rate multiplied by the quantity supplied.

a. Taxation as slavery
b. Taxable wage
c. Tax and spend
d. Tax revenue

9. From a Keynesian point of view, a _________ in the public sector is achieved when the government equates the revenues with expenditure over the business cycles. In other words, a government's budget is balanced if its income is equal to its expenditure. It is a budget in which revenues are equal to spending.

a. Budget support
b. Budget crisis
c. Budget theory
d. Balanced budget

10. A _________ is a situation in which the government takes in more than it spends.

a. 100-year flood
b. Budget set
c. 130-30 fund
d. Budget surplus

11. _________s is the social science that studies the production, distribution, and consumption of goods and services. The term _________s comes from the Ancient Greek oá¼°κονομÎ¯α from oá¼¶κος (oikos, 'house') + νÏŒμος (nomos, 'custom' or 'law'), hence 'rules of the house(hold)'. Current _________ models developed out of the broader field of political economy in the late 19th century, owing to a desire to use an empirical approach more akin to the physical sciences.

a. Opportunity cost
b. Inflation
c. Economic
d. Energy economics

12. _________ is the increase in the amount of the goods and services produced by an economy over time. It is conventionally measured as the percent rate of increase in real gross domestic product, or real GDP. Growth is usually calculated in real terms, i.e. inflation-adjusted terms, in order to net out the effect of inflation on the price of the goods and services produced.

a. ACEA agreement
b. AD-IA Model
c. ACCRA Cost of Living Index
d. Economic growth

13. The _________ was a worldwide economic downturn starting in most places in 1929 and ending at different times in the 1930s or early 1940s for different countries. It was the largest and most important economic depression in the 20th century, and is used in the 21st century as an example of how far the world's economy can fall. The _________ originated in the United States; historians most often use as a starting date the stock market crash on October 29, 1929, known as Black Tuesday.

a. Wall Street Crash of 1929
b. British Empire Economic Conference
c. Jarrow March
d. Great Depression

14. _________, 1st Baron Keynes was a renowned economist from Britain whose many ideas on economic and political theories as well as on many governments' monetary policies influenced America. He advocated a government that played an active role in the lives of people regarding business, economy, etc. In this role, the government would use fiscal measures to reduce the consequences of recessions, economic depressions and booms.

a. Adam Smith
b. Adolf Hitler
c. Adolph Fischer
d. John Maynard Keynes

15. _________ and Keynesian Theory) is a macroeconomic theory based on the ideas of 20th-century British economist John Maynard Keynes. _________ argues that private sector decisions sometimes lead to inefficient macroeconomic outcomes and therefore advocates active policy responses by the public sector, including monetary policy actions by the central bank and fiscal policy actions by the government to stabilize output over the business cycle.

The theories forming the basis of _________ were first presented in The General Theory of Employment, Interest and Money, published in 1936.

a. Keynesian economics
b. Deflation
c. Rational choice theory
d. Market failure

16. In finance and economics _________ or nominal rate of interest refers to the rate of interest before adjustment for inflation (in contrast with the real interest rate); or, for interest rates 'as stated' without adjustment for the full effect of compounding (also referred to as the nominal annual rate.) An interest rate is called nominal if the frequency of compounding (e.g. a month) is not identical to the basic time unit (normally a year.)

The real interest rate includes compensation for the lender's lost value due to inflation, whereas the _________ excludes inflation.

a. Risk-free interest rate
b. London Interbank Offered Rate
c. Fixed interest
d. Nominal interest rate

17. _________ is a fee paid on borrowed assets. It is the price paid for the use of borrowed money , or, money earned by deposited funds . Assets that are sometimes lent with _________ include money, shares, consumer goods through hire purchase, major assets such as aircraft, and even entire factories in finance lease arrangements.

a. Insolvency
b. Interest
c. Internal debt
d. Asset protection

18. An _________ is the price a borrower pays for the use of money they do not own, for instance a small company might borrow from a bank to kick start their business, and the return a lender receives for deferring the use of funds, by lending it to the borrower. _________s are normally expressed as a percentage rate over the period of one year.

_________s targets are also a vital tool of monetary policy and are used to control variables like investment, inflation, and unemployment.

a. Enterprise value
b. Arrow-Debreu model
c. ACCRA Cost of Living Index
d. Interest rate

19. In economics, _________ is the use of government spending and revenue collection to influence the economy.

_________ can be contrasted with the other main type of economic policy, monetary policy, which attempts to stabilize the economy by controlling interest rates and the supply of money. The two main instruments of _________ are government spending and taxation.

a. 100-year flood
b. Fiscalism
c. Sustainable investment rule
d. Fiscal policy

20. An _________, in economics, is the amount by which the real Gross domestic product exceeds potential GDP. The real GDP is also known as GDP 'adjusted for inflation', 'constant prices' GDP or 'constant dollar' GDP, because it measures the aggregate output in a country's income accounts in a given year, expressed in base-year prices. On the other hand, the potential GDP is the quantity of real GDP when a country's economy is at full-employment.

a. ACEA agreement
b. AD-IA Model
c. Inflationary gap
d. ACCRA Cost of Living Index

21. The GDP gap or the output gap is the difference between potential GDP and actual GDP or actual output. The calculation for the output gap is Y-Y* where Y* is potential output and Y is actual output. If this calculation yields a positive number it is called an expansionary gap and indicates an economy in expansion; if the calculation yields a negative number it is called a _________ and indicates an economy in recession.

a. 100-year flood
b. 1921 recession
c. Recessionary gap
d. 130-30 fund

22. An _________ is a tax levied on the financial income of people, corporations, or other legal entities. Various _________ systems exist, with varying degrees of tax incidence. Income taxation can be progressive, proportional, or regressive.

a. ACCRA Cost of Living Index
b. Income tax
c. ACEA agreement
d. AD-IA Model

23. In economics, a _________ is a general slowdown in economic activity over a sustained period of time, or a business cycle contraction. During _________s, many macroeconomic indicators vary in a similar way. Production as measured by Gross Domestic Product (GDP), employment, investment spending, capacity utilization, household incomes and business profits all fall during _________s.

a. Monetary economics
b. Leading indicators
c. Treasury View
d. Recession

24. _________ is the process by which the government, central bank (ii) availability of money, and (iii) cost of money or rate of interest, in order to attain a set of objectives oriented towards the growth and stability of the economy. Monetary theory provides insight into how to craft optimal _________.

_________ is referred to as either being an expansionary policy where an expansionary policy increases the total supply of money in the economy, and a contractionary policy decreases the total money supply.

a. Monetary policy
b. 100-year flood
c. 130-30 fund
d. 1921 recession

25. In economics, _________ is the total demand for final goods and services in the economy (Y) at a given time and price level. It is the amount of goods and services in the economy that will be purchased at all possible price levels. This is the demand for the gross domestic product of a country when inventory levels are static.

a. Aggregate demand
b. Aggregate expenditure
c. Aggregate supply
d. Aggregation problem

26. _________ is that which is owed; usually referencing assets owed, but the term can also cover moral obligations and other interactions not requiring money. In the case of assets, _________ is a means of using future purchasing power in the present before a summation has been earned. Some companies and corporations use _________ as a part of their overall corporate finance strategy.

a. Debt
b. Collateral Management
c. Hard money loan
d. Debenture

27. Economics:

- _________,the desire to own something and the ability to pay for it
- _________ curve,a graphic representation of a _________ schedule
- _________ deposit, the money in checking accounts
- _________ pull theory,the theory that inflation occurs when _________ for goods and services exceeds existing supplies
- _________ schedule,a table that lists the quantity of a good a person will buy it each different price
- _________ side economics,the school of economics at believes government spending and tax cuts open economy by raising _________

.

a. McKesson ' Robbins scandal
b. Demand
c. Production
d. Variability

28. The _________ or gross domestic income (GDI), a basic measure of an economy's economic performance, is the market value of all final goods and services produced within the borders of a nation in a year. _________ can be defined in three ways, all of which are conceptually identical. First, it is equal to the total expenditures for all final goods and services produced within the country in a stipulated period of time (usually a 365-day year.)

a. Countercyclical
b. Monopolistic competition
c. Market structure
d. Gross domestic product

1. Economics:

- _________,the desire to own something and the ability to pay for it
- _________ curve,a graphic representation of a _________ schedule
- _________ deposit, the money in checking accounts
- _________ pull theory,the theory that inflation occurs when _________ for goods and services exceeds existing supplies
- _________ schedule,a table that lists the quantity of a good a person will buy it each different price
- _________ side economics,the school of economics at believes government spending and tax cuts open economy by raising _________

.

a. Variability
b. Production
c. McKesson ' Robbins scandal
d. Demand

2. _________ is a type of bank account where the money in the account is legally able to be withdrawn immediately upon demand (or 'at call'.) This type of bank account can also be referred to as a 'cheque' or 'checking' or transactional account.

This type of bank account, allowing immediate conversion of the account balance into cash or withdrawal to another account, can be contrasted with a time deposit (also known as a certificate of deposit or term deposit), where the funds are not legally available for immediate withdrawal by the depositor.

a. Tangible Common Equity
b. Debt rescheduling
c. Clawbacks in economic development
d. Demand deposit

3. A _________ is an intermediary used in trade to avoid the inconveniences of a pure barter system.

By contrast, as William Stanley Jevons argued, in a barter system there must be a coincidence of wants before two people can trade - one must want exactly what the other has to offer, when and where it is offered, so that the exchange can occur. A _________ permits the value of goods to be assessed and rendered in terms of the intermediary, most often, a form of money widely accepted to buy any other good.

a. Consumer theory
b. Medium of exchange
c. Price revolution
d. Labour economics

4. To act as a _________, a commodity, a form of money stored, and retrieved - and be predictably useful when it is so retrieved.

This is distinct from the standard of deferred payment function which requires acceptability to parties one owes a debt to and a minimum of opportunity to cheat others.

a. Store of value
b. Petrodollar
c. World currency
d. Fiat money

5. In financial accounting, a _________ or statement of financial position is a summary of a person's or organization's balances. Assets, liabilities and ownership equity are listed as of a specific date, such as the end of its financial year. A _________ is often described as a snapshot of a company's financial condition.

a. 100-year flood
b. 1921 recession
c. 130-30 fund
d. Balance sheet

6. _________ is a term used in economics to describe highly liquid assets that can easily be converted into cash.

Various sources provide the following examples of _________:

- Savings account
- Money funds
- Bank time deposits (Certificates of deposit)
- Government treasury securities (such as T-bills)
- Bonds near their redemption date
- Foreign currencies, especially widely traded ones such as the US dollar, euro or yen.
- list of countries by stocks of quasi money.

.

a. Silver standard
b. Monetary base
c. Near Money
d. Veil of money

7. _________ is the a method of technical and economic research of the systems for purpose to optimize a parity between system's consumer functions or properties and expenses to achieve those functions or properties.

This methodology for continuous perfection of production, industrial technologies, organizational structures was developed by Juryj Sobolev in 1948 at the 'Perm telephone factory'

- 1948 Juryj Sobolev - the first success in application of a method analysis at the 'Perm telephone factory' .
- 1949 - the first application for the invention as result of use of the new method.

Today in economically developed countries practically each enterprise or the company use methodology of the kind of functional-cost analysis as a practice of the quality management, most full satisfying to principles of standards of series ISO 9000.

- Interest of consumer not in products itself, but the advantage which it will receive from its usage.
- The consumer aspires to reduce his expenses
- Functions needed by consumer can be executed in the various ways, and, hence, with various efficiency and expenses. Among possible alternatives of realization of functions exist such in which the parity of quality and the price is the optimal for the consumer.

The goal of _________ is achievement of the highest consumer satisfaction of production at simultaneous decrease in all kinds of industrial expenses Classical _________ has three English synonyms - Value Engineering, Value Management, Value Analysis.

a. Willingness to pay
b. Staple financing
c. Monopoly wage
d. Function cost analysis

8. In business and accounting, _________ are everything of value that is owned by a person or company. It is a claim on the property your income of a borrower. The balance sheet of a firm records the monetary value of the _________ owned by the firm.

a. ACEA agreement
b. ACCRA Cost of Living Index
c. Amortization schedule
d. Assets

9. A _________ is a professionally managed type of collective investment scheme that pools money from many investors and invests it in stocks, bonds, short-term money market instruments, and/or other securities. The _________ will have a fund manager that trades the pooled money on a regular basis. As of early 2008, the worldwide value of all _________s totals more than $26 trillion.

a. Mutual fund
b. Self-invested personal pension
c. Dark pools of liquidity
d. Participating policy

10. _________ is the revenue to a brokerage firm when commissioned securities and insurance salespeople sell a product, whether it is an investment like stocks, bonds or insurance like life insurance or long term care insurance. The commission that the agent receives is usually a percentage of this figure, although some firms like Merrill Lynch use figures called Production Credits, usually smaller than _________, to determine payouts and retain more revenue.

For example, a mutual fund with a 5.75% sales charge is sold to someone who invests $10,000.

a. Monopoly price
b. Discretionary policy
c. Number of Shares
d. Gross Dealer Concession

11. In economics, _________ is the total amount of money available in an economy at a particular point in time. There are several ways to define 'money', but standard measures usually include currency in circulation and demand deposits.

_________ data are recorded and published, usually by the government or the central bank of the country.

a. Neutrality of money
b. Money supply
c. Velocity of money
d. Veil of money

12. Discounting is a financial mechanism in which a debtor obtains the right to delay payments to a creditor, for a defined period of time, in exchange for a charge or fee. Essentially, the party that owes money in the present purchases the right to delay the payment until some future date. The _________, or charge, is simply the difference between the original amount owed in the present and the amount that has to be paid in the future to settle the debt.

a. Discount
b. Reliability theory
c. Certified Risk Manager
d. Reinsurance

13. The _________ is an interest rate a central bank charges depository institutions that borrow reserves from it.

The term _________ has two meanings:

- the same as interest rate; the term 'discount' does not refer to the meaning of the word, but to the purpose of using the quantity, such as computations of present value, e.g. net present value or discounted cash flow

- the annual effective _________, which is the annual interest divided by the capital including that interest; this rate is lower than the interest rate; it corresponds to using the value after a year as the nominal value, and seeing the initial value as the nominal value minus a discount; it is used for Treasury Bills and similar financial instruments

The annual effective _________ is the annual interest divided by the capital including that interest, which is the interest rate divided by 100% plus the interest rate. It is the annual discount factor to be applied to the future cash flow, to find the discount, subtracted from a future value to find the value one year earlier.

For example, suppose there is a government bond that sells for $95 and pays $100 in a year's time.

a. Discount rate
b. Perpetuity
c. Johansen test
d. Stochastic volatility

14. In banking, _________ are bank reserves in excess of the reserve requirement set by a central bank (in the United States, the Federal Reserve System, called the Fed; in Canada, the Bank of Canada.) They are reserves of cash more than the required amounts. Holding _________ is generally considered costly and uneconomical as no interest is earned on the excess amount.

a. Origination fee
b. Annual percentage rate
c. Universal bank
d. Excess reserves

15. The accounting equation relates assets, _________, and owner's equity:

Assets = _________ + Owner's Equity

The accounting equation is the mathematical structure of the balance sheet.

The Australian Accounting Research Foundation defines _________ as: 'future sacrifice of economic benefits that the entity is presently obliged to make to other entities as a result of past transactions and other past events.'

Probably the most accepted accounting definition of liability is the one used by the International Accounting Standards Board (IASB.) The following is a quotation from IFRS Framework:

A liability is a present obligation of the enterprise arising from past events, the settlement of which is expected to result in an outflow from the enterprise of resources embodying economic benefits

-

Regulations as to the recognition of _________ are different all over the world, but are roughly similar to those of the IASB.

a. Coase theorem
b. Liabilities
c. Community property
d. Competition law theory

16. The _________ is a bank regulation that sets the minimum reserves each bank must hold to customer deposits and notes. It would normally be in the form of fiat currency stored in a bank vault (vault cash), or with a central bank.

The reserve ratio is sometimes used as a tool in the monetary policy, influencing the country's economy, borrowing, and interest rates.

a. Reserve requirement
b. Fractional-reserve banking
c. Probability of default
d. Private money

17. _________ is the concept or idea of fairness in economics, particularly as to taxation or welfare economics.

In welfare economics, _________ may be distinguished from economic efficiency in overall evaluation of social welfare. Although '_________' has broader uses, it may be posed as a counterpart to economic inequality in yielding a 'good' distribution of welfare.

a. ACCRA Cost of Living Index
b. Equity
c. ACEA agreement
d. AD-IA Model

18. The _________ is the central bank of the United Kingdom and is the model on which most modern, large central banks have been based. Since 1946 it has been a state-owned institution. It was established in 1694 to act as the English Government's banker, and to this day it still acts as the banker for the UK Government.

a. Bank of England
b. 130-30 fund
c. 100-year flood
d. 1921 recession

19. A _________, reserve bank, or monetary authority is the entity responsible for the monetary policy of a country or of a group of member states. It is a bank that can lend money to other banks in times of need. Its primary responsibility is to maintain the stability of the national currency and money supply, but more active duties include controlling subsidized-loan interest rates, and acting as a lender of last resort to the banking sector during times of financial crisis (private banks often being integral to the national financial system.)

a. Central bank
b. 100-year flood
c. 1921 recession
d. 130-30 fund

20. The term _________ refers to government debt, expenditures and revenues, or to finance (particularly financial revenue) in general.

- _________ deficit is the budget deficit of federal or local government
- _________ policy is the discretionary spending of governments. Contrasts with monetary policy.
- _________ year and _________ quarter are reporting periods for firms and other agencies.

.

a. Procter ' Gamble
b. Bucket shop
c. Drawdown
d. Fiscal

21. In economics, _________ is the use of government spending and revenue collection to influence the economy.

_________ can be contrasted with the other main type of economic policy, monetary policy, which attempts to stabilize the economy by controlling interest rates and the supply of money. The two main instruments of _________ are government spending and taxation.

a. 100-year flood
b. Fiscal policy
c. Fiscalism
d. Sustainable investment rule

22. The Federal Reserve System (also the Federal Reserve; informally The Fed) is the central banking system of the United States. Created in 1913 by the enactment of the Federal Reserve Act (signed by Woodrow Wilson), it is a quasi-public and quasi-private (government entity with private components) banking system that comprises (1) the presidentially appointed Board of Governors of the Federal Reserve System in Washington, D.C.; (2) the Federal Open Market Committee; (3) twelve regional _________ located in major cities throughout the nation acting as fiscal agents for the U.S. Treasury, each with its own nine-member board of directors; (4) numerous other private U.S. member banks, which subscribe to required amounts of non-transferable stock in their regional _________; and (5) various advisory councils. Since February 2006, Ben Bernanke has served as the Chairman of the Board of Governors of the Federal Reserve System.

a. Federal Reserve banks
b. Federal funds
c. Fed Funds Probability
d. Federal Open Market Committee

23. The _________ consists of a number of economic theories which describe the nature of the firm, company including its existence, its behaviour, and its relationship with the market.

In simplified terms, the _________ aims to answer these questions:

1. Existence - why do firms emerge, why are not all transactions in the economy mediated over the market?
2. Boundaries - why the boundary between firms and the market is located exactly there? Which transactions are performed internally and which are negotiated on the market?
3. Organization - why are firms structured in such specific way? What is the interplay of formal and informal relationships?

Despite looking simple, these questions are not answered by the established economic theory, which usually views firms as given, and treats them as black boxes without any internal structure.

The First World War period saw a change of emphasis in economic theory away from industry-level analysis which mainly included analysing markets to analysis at the level of the firm, as it became increasingly clear that perfect competition was no longer an adequate model of how firms behaved. Economic theory till then had focussed on trying to understand markets alone and there had been little study on understanding why firms or organisations exist.

a. Technology gap
b. Khazzoom-Brookes postulate
c. Policy Ineffectiveness Proposition
d. Theory of the firm

24. The _________ is a United States government corporation created by the Glass-Steagall Act of 1933. It provides deposit insurance, which guarantees the safety of deposits in member banks, currently up to $250,000 per depositor per bank. Funds in non-interest bearing transaction accounts are fully insured, with no limit, under the temporary Transaction Account Guarantee Program.

a. Luxembourg Income Study
b. Foreign direct investment
c. Great Leap Forward
d. Federal Deposit Insurance Corporation

25. The _________ , a component of the Federal Reserve System, is charged under United States law with overseeing the nation's open market operations. It is the Federal Reserve Committee that makes key decisions about interest rates and the growth jam of the United States money supply. It is the principal organ of United States national monetary policy.

a. Primary Dealer Credit Facility
b. Fed Funds Probability
c. Federal Open Market Committee
d. Federal Reserve Transparency Act

26. _________, in law and economics, is a form of risk management primarily used to hedge against the risk of a contingent loss. _________ is defined as the equitable transfer of the risk of a loss, from one entity to another, in exchange for a premium, and can be thought of as a guaranteed small loss to prevent a large, possibly devastating loss. An insurer is a company selling the _________; an insured or policyholder is the person or entity buying the _________.

a. Insurance
b. ACEA agreement
c. AD-IA Model
d. ACCRA Cost of Living Index

27. In economics, the _________ is the term used to refer to the environment in which bonds are bought and sold between a central bank ' its regulated banks. It is not a free market process.

- To intervene in the 'business cycle', a central bank may choose to go into the _________ and buy or sell government bonds, which is known as _________ operations to increase reserves.

a. Open Market
b. Outside money
c. ACCRA Cost of Living Index
d. Inside money

28. _________ is the process by which the government, central bank (ii) availability of money, and (iii) cost of money or rate of interest, in order to attain a set of objectives oriented towards the growth and stability of the economy. Monetary theory provides insight into how to craft optimal _________.

_________ is referred to as either being an expansionary policy where an expansionary policy increases the total supply of money in the economy, and a contractionary policy decreases the total money supply.

a. 1921 recession
b. 130-30 fund
c. 100-year flood
d. Monetary policy

29. A security is a fungible, negotiable instrument representing financial value. _________ are broadly categorized into debt _________; equity _________, e.g., common stocks; and derivative (finance) contracts such as forwards, futures, options and swaps. The company or other entity issuing the security is called the issuer.

a. Red herring prospectus
b. Pass-Through Certificates
c. Securities
d. Settlement risk

30. In the United States, _________ are overnight borrowings by banks to maintain their bank reserves at the Federal Reserve. Banks keep reserves at Federal Reserve Banks to meet their reserve requirements and to clear financial transactions. Transactions in the _________ market enable depository institutions with reserve balances in excess of reserve requirements to lend reserves to institutions with reserve deficiencies.

a. Term auction facility
b. Federal funds rate
c. Federal funds
d. Federal Reserve Transparency Act

31. In the United States, the _________ is the interest rate at which private depository institutions (mostly banks) lend balances (federal funds) at the Federal Reserve to other depository institutions, usually overnight. It is the interest rate banks charge each other for loans. Changing the target rate is one way the Chairman of the Federal Reserve can influence the supply of money in the U.S. economy..

a. Term auction facility
b. Monetary Policy Report to the Congress
c. Federal banking
d. Federal funds rate

32. _________ is a fee paid on borrowed assets. It is the price paid for the use of borrowed money , or, money earned by deposited funds . Assets that are sometimes lent with _________ include money, shares, consumer goods through hire purchase, major assets such as aircraft, and even entire factories in finance lease arrangements.

a. Internal debt
b. Asset protection
c. Insolvency
d. Interest

33. An _________ is the price a borrower pays for the use of money they do not own, for instance a small company might borrow from a bank to kick start their business, and the return a lender receives for deferring the use of funds, by lending it to the borrower. _________s are normally expressed as a percentage rate over the period of one year.

_________s targets are also a vital tool of monetary policy and are used to control variables like investment, inflation, and unemployment.

a. Enterprise value
b. Interest rate
c. ACCRA Cost of Living Index
d. Arrow-Debreu model

34. In economics, _________ is the total demand for final goods and services in the economy (Y) at a given time and price level. It is the amount of goods and services in the economy that will be purchased at all possible price levels. This is the demand for the gross domestic product of a country when inventory levels are static.

a. Aggregate expenditure
b. Aggregate demand
c. Aggregation problem
d. Aggregate supply

35. In economics, the _________ can be defined as the graph depicting the relationship between the price of a certain commodity, and the amount of it that consumers are willing and able to purchase at that given price. It is a graphic representation of a demand schedule. The _________ for all consumers together follows from the _________ of every individual consumer: the individual demands at each price are added together.

a. Cost curve
b. Kuznets curve
c. Wage curve
d. Demand curve

36. The _________ is the desired holding of money balances in the form of cash or bank deposits.

Money is dominated as store of value by interest bearing assets. However, money is necessary to carry out transactions, or in other words, it provides liquidity.

a. Conglomerate merger
b. Demand for Money
c. Borrowing base
d. Market neutral

37. _________s is the social science that studies the production, distribution, and consumption of goods and services. The term _________s comes from the Ancient Greek oá¼°κονομΐ¯α from oá¼¶κος (oikos, 'house') + νΐŒμος (nomos, 'custom' or 'law'), hence 'rules of the house(hold)'. Current _________ models developed out of the broader field of political economy in the late 19th century, owing to a desire to use an empirical approach more akin to the physical sciences.

a. Inflation
b. Economic
c. Energy economics
d. Opportunity cost

38. _________ is an American economist and was the Chairman of the Federal Reserve of the United States from 1987 to 2006. He currently works as a private advisor and providing consulting for firms through his company, Greenspan Associates LLC.

First appointed Federal Reserve chairman by President Ronald Reagan in August 1987, he was reappointed at successive four-year intervals until retiring on January 31, 2006 after the second-longest tenure in the position.

a. Adolf Hitler
b. Adolph Fischer
c. Adam Smith
d. Alan Greenspan

1. The term _________ refers to government debt, expenditures and revenues, or to finance (particularly financial revenue) in general.

- _________ deficit is the budget deficit of federal or local government
- _________ policy is the discretionary spending of governments. Contrasts with monetary policy.
- _________ year and _________ quarter are reporting periods for firms and other agencies.

.

a. Bucket shop
b. Fiscal
c. Drawdown
d. Procter ' Gamble

2. In economics, _________ is the use of government spending and revenue collection to influence the economy.

_________ can be contrasted with the other main type of economic policy, monetary policy, which attempts to stabilize the economy by controlling interest rates and the supply of money. The two main instruments of _________ are government spending and taxation.

a. Sustainable investment rule
b. 100-year flood
c. Fiscal policy
d. Fiscalism

3. _________ is the process by which the government, central bank (ii) availability of money, and (iii) cost of money or rate of interest, in order to attain a set of objectives oriented towards the growth and stability of the economy. Monetary theory provides insight into how to craft optimal _________.

_________ is referred to as either being an expansionary policy where an expansionary policy increases the total supply of money in the economy, and a contractionary policy decreases the total money supply.

a. 1921 recession
b. 130-30 fund
c. Monetary policy
d. 100-year flood

4. Discounting is a financial mechanism in which a debtor obtains the right to delay payments to a creditor, for a defined period of time, in exchange for a charge or fee. Essentially, the party that owes money in the present purchases the right to delay the payment until some future date. The _________, or charge, is simply the difference between the original amount owed in the present and the amount that has to be paid in the future to settle the debt.

a. Certified Risk Manager
b. Reinsurance
c. Reliability theory
d. Discount

5. The _________ is an interest rate a central bank charges depository institutions that borrow reserves from it.

The term _________ has two meanings:

- the same as interest rate; the term 'discount' does not refer to the meaning of the word, but to the purpose of using the quantity, such as computations of present value, e.g. net present value or discounted cash flow

- the annual effective _________, which is the annual interest divided by the capital including that interest; this rate is lower than the interest rate; it corresponds to using the value after a year as the nominal value, and seeing the initial value as the nominal value minus a discount; it is used for Treasury Bills and similar financial instruments

The annual effective _________ is the annual interest divided by the capital including that interest, which is the interest rate divided by 100% plus the interest rate. It is the annual discount factor to be applied to the future cash flow, to find the discount, subtracted from a future value to find the value one year earlier.

For example, suppose there is a government bond that sells for $95 and pays $100 in a year's time.

a. Perpetuity
b. Johansen test
c. Discount rate
d. Stochastic volatility

6. _________s is the social science that studies the production, distribution, and consumption of goods and services. The term _________s comes from the Ancient Greek οá¼°κονομÎ¯α from οá¼¶κος (oikos, 'house') + νÏŒμος (nomos, 'custom' or 'law'), hence 'rules of the house(hold)'. Current _________ models developed out of the broader field of political economy in the late 19th century, owing to a desire to use an empirical approach more akin to the physical sciences.

a. Energy economics
b. Economic
c. Inflation
d. Opportunity cost

7. _________, 1st Baron Keynes was a renowned economist from Britain whose many ideas on economic and political theories as well as on many governments' monetary policies influenced America. He advocated a government that played an active role in the lives of people regarding business, economy, etc. In this role, the government would use fiscal measures to reduce the consequences of recessions, economic depressions and booms.

a. John Maynard Keynes
b. Adam Smith
c. Adolph Fischer
d. Adolf Hitler

8. _________ and Keynesian Theory) is a macroeconomic theory based on the ideas of 20th-century British economist John Maynard Keynes. _________ argues that private sector decisions sometimes lead to inefficient macroeconomic outcomes and therefore advocates active policy responses by the public sector, including monetary policy actions by the central bank and fiscal policy actions by the government to stabilize output over the business cycle.

The theories forming the basis of _________ were first presented in The General Theory of Employment, Interest and Money, published in 1936.

a. Rational choice theory
b. Keynesian economics
c. Market failure
d. Deflation

9. _________ is one of the four Ps of the marketing mix. The other three aspects are product, promotion, and place. It is also a key variable in microeconomic price allocation theory.

a. Point of total assumption
b. Premium pricing
c. Guaranteed Maximum Price
d. Pricing

10. _________ is the view within monetary economics that variation in the money supply has major influences on national output in the short run and the price level over longer periods and that objectives of monetary policy are best met by targeting the growth rate of the money supply.

_________ today is mainly associated with the work of Milton Friedman, who was among the generation of economists to accept Keynesian economics and then criticize it on his own terms. Friedman and Anna Schwartz wrote an influential book, Monetary History of the United States 1867-1960, and argued that 'inflation is always and everywhere a monetary phenomenon.' Friedman advocated a central bank policy aimed at keeping the supply and demand for money at equilibrium, as measured by growth in productivity and demand.

a. Marginal revenue productivity theory of wages
b. Complexity economics
c. Monetarism
d. Historical school of economics

11. In finance and economics _________ or nominal rate of interest refers to the rate of interest before adjustment for inflation (in contrast with the real interest rate); or, for interest rates 'as stated' without adjustment for the full effect of compounding (also referred to as the nominal annual rate.) An interest rate is called nominal if the frequency of compounding (e.g. a month) is not identical to the basic time unit (normally a year.)

The real interest rate includes compensation for the lender's lost value due to inflation, whereas the _________ excludes inflation.

a. Risk-free interest rate
b. London Interbank Offered Rate
c. Nominal interest rate
d. Fixed interest

12. _________ is a fee paid on borrowed assets. It is the price paid for the use of borrowed money , or, money earned by deposited funds . Assets that are sometimes lent with _________ include money, shares, consumer goods through hire purchase, major assets such as aircraft, and even entire factories in finance lease arrangements.

a. Insolvency
b. Internal debt
c. Asset protection
d. Interest

13. An _________ is the price a borrower pays for the use of money they do not own, for instance a small company might borrow from a bank to kick start their business, and the return a lender receives for deferring the use of funds, by lending it to the borrower. _________s are normally expressed as a percentage rate over the period of one year.

_________s targets are also a vital tool of monetary policy and are used to control variables like investment, inflation, and unemployment.

a. ACCRA Cost of Living Index
b. Arrow-Debreu model
c. Enterprise value
d. Interest rate

14. A _________ is:

- Rewrite _________, in generative grammar and computer science
- Standardization, a formal and widely-accepted statement, fact, definition, or qualification
- Operation, a determinate _________ for performing a mathematical operation and obtaining a certain result (Mathematics, Logic)
    - Unary operation
    - Binary operation
- _________ of inference, a function from sets of formulae to formulae (Mathematics, Logic)
- _________ of thumb, principle with broad application that is not intended to be strictly accurate or reliable for every situation. Also often simply referred to as a _________
- Moral, an atomic element of a moral code for guiding choices in human behavior
- Heuristic, a quantized '_________' which shows a tendency or probability for successful function
- A regulation, as in sports
- A Production _________, as in computer science
- Procedural law, a _________set governing the application of laws to cases
    - A law, which may informally be called a '_________'
    - A court ruling, a decision by a court
- In the U.S. Government, a regulation mandated by Congress, but written or expanded upon by the Executive Branch.
- Norm (sociology), an informal but widely accepted _________, concept, truth, definition, or qualification (social norms, legal norms, coding norms)
- Norm (philosophy), a kind of sentence or a reason to act, feel or believe
- 'Rulership' is the concept of governance by a government:
    - Military _________, governance by a military body
    - Monastic _________, a collection of precepts that guides the life of monks or nuns in a religious order where the superior holds the place of Christ
- Slide _________

- '_________,' a song by Ayumi Hamasaki
- '_________,' a song by rapper Nas
- '_________s,' an album by the band The Whitest Boy Alive
- _________s: Pyaar Ka Superhit Formula, a 2003 Bollywood film
- ruler, an instrument for measuring lengths
- _________, a component of an astrolabe, circumferator or similar instrument
- The _________s, a bestselling self-help book
- _________ Project (Run Up-to-date Linux Everywhere), a project that aims to use up-to-date Linux software on old PCs
- _________ engine, a software system that helps managing business _________s
- Ja _________, a hip hop artist
    - R.U.L.E., a 2005 greatest hits album by rapper Ja _________
- '_________s,' a KMFDM song

a. Technocracy
b. Procter ' Gamble
c. Rule
d. Demand

15. _________ was an American economist, statistician and public intellectual, and a recipient of the Nobel Memorial Prize in Economic Sciences. He is best known among scholars for his theoretical and empirical research, especially consumption analysis, monetary history and theory, and for his demonstration of the complexity of stabilization policy. A global public followed his restatement of a political philosophy that insisted on minimizing the role of government in favor of the private sector.

a. Adolph Fischer
b. Adam Smith
c. Adolf Hitler
d. Milton Friedman

16. The _________ was a worldwide economic downturn starting in most places in 1929 and ending at different times in the 1930s or early 1940s for different countries. It was the largest and most important economic depression in the 20th century, and is used in the 21st century as an example of how far the world's economy can fall. The _________ originated in the United States; historians most often use as a starting date the stock market crash on October 29, 1929, known as Black Tuesday.

a. British Empire Economic Conference
b. Jarrow March
c. Great Depression
d. Wall Street Crash of 1929

17. In economics and especially in the theory of competition, _________ are obstacles in the path of a firm that make it difficult to enter a given market.

_________ are the source of a firm's pricing power - the ability of a firm to raise prices without losing all its customers.

The term refers to hindrances that an individual may face while trying to gain entrance into a profession or trade.

a. Social dumping
b. Group boycott
c. Limit price
d. Barriers to entry

18. _________ in economics and business is the result of an exchange and from that trade we assign a numerical monetary value to a good, service or asset. If Alice trades Bob 4 apples for an orange, the _________ of an orange is 4 apples. Inversely, the _________ of an apple is 1/4 oranges.

a. Price war
b. Premium pricing
c. Price book
d. Price

19. In economics, _________ is the total demand for final goods and services in the economy (Y) at a given time and price level. It is the amount of goods and services in the economy that will be purchased at all possible price levels. This is the demand for the gross domestic product of a country when inventory levels are static.

a. Aggregation problem
b. Aggregate expenditure
c. Aggregate supply
d. Aggregate demand

20. In economics, _________ is the total supply of goods and services produced by a national economy during a specific time period. It is the total amount of goods and services in the economy available at all possible price levels.

a. Aggregation problem
b. Aggregate expenditure
c. Aggregate supply
d. Aggregate demand

21. Economics:

- _________,the desire to own something and the ability to pay for it
- _________ curve,a graphic representation of a _________ schedule
- _________ deposit, the money in checking accounts
- _________ pull theory,the theory that inflation occurs when _________ for goods and services exceeds existing supplies
- _________ schedule,a table that lists the quantity of a good a person will buy it each different price
- _________ side economics,the school of economics at believes government spending and tax cuts open economy by raising _________

.

a. Variability
b. Production
c. McKesson ' Robbins scandal
d. Demand

22. _________ is an assumption used in many contemporary macroeconomic models, and also in other areas of contemporary economics and game theory and in other applications of rational choice theory.

Since most macroeconomic models today study decisions over many periods, the expectations of workers, consumers, and firms about future economic conditions are an essential part of the model. How to model these expectations has long been controversial, and it is well known that the macroeconomic predictions of the model may differ depending on the assumptions made about expectations

a. Minimum wage
b. Potential output
c. Balanced-growth equilibrium
d. Rational expectations

23. _________ is a term used to describe macroeconomic policy based on the ad hoc judgment of policymakers as opposed to policy set by predetermined rules. For instance, a central banker could make decisions on interest rates on a case by case basis instead of allowing a set rule, such as the Taylor rule, determine interest rates.

Discretionary policies are similar to 'feedback-rule policies' used by the Federal Reserve to achieve price level stability.

a. Demand for money
b. Boom and bust
c. Discretionary policy
d. Managerial economics

24. A _________ is a normalized average (typically a weighted average) of prices for a given class of goods or services in a given region, during a given interval of time. It is a statistic designed to help to compare how these prices, taken as a whole, differ between time periods or geographical locations.

Price indices have several potential uses.

a. Two-part tariff
b. Transactional Net Margin Method
c. Price Index
d. Product sabotage

25. A _________ measures average changes in prices received by domestic producers for their output. It is one of several price indices

Its importance is being undermined by the steady decline in manufactured goods as a share of spending.

A number of countries that now report a _________ previously reported a Wholesale Price Index.

a. Gross national product
b. Hemline index
c. Visible balance
d. Producer Price Index

26. _________ is a school of macroeconomic thought that argues that economic growth can be most effectively created using incentives for people to produce (supply) goods and services, such as adjusting income tax and capital gains tax rates, and by allowing greater flexibility by reducing regulation. Consumers will then benefit from a greater supply of goods and services at lower prices.

The term _________ was coined by journalist Jude Wanniski in 1975, and popularized the ideas of economists Robert Mundell and Arthur Laffer.

a. Fiscal stimulus plans
b. Commodity trading advisors
c. Clap note
d. Supply-side economics

27. _________ is the increase in the amount of the goods and services produced by an economy over time. It is conventionally measured as the percent rate of increase in real gross domestic product, or real GDP. Growth is usually calculated in real terms, i.e. inflation-adjusted terms, in order to net out the effect of inflation on the price of the goods and services produced.

a. ACCRA Cost of Living Index
b. AD-IA Model
c. ACEA agreement
d. Economic growth

28. In economics, a _________ is a general slowdown in economic activity over a sustained period of time, or a business cycle contraction. During _________s, many macroeconomic indicators vary in a similar way. Production as measured by Gross Domestic Product (GDP), employment, investment spending, capacity utilization, household incomes and business profits all fall during _________s.

a. Monetary economics
b. Treasury View
c. Leading indicators
d. Recession

29. To _________ is to impose a financial charge or other levy upon a taxpayer by a state or the functional equivalent of a state.

_________es are also imposed by many subnational entities. _________es consist of direct _________ or indirect _________, and may be paid in money or as its labour equivalent (often but not always unpaid.)

a. 1921 recession
b. 130-30 fund
c. 100-year flood
d. Tax

1. The _________ or gross domestic income (GDI), a basic measure of an economy's economic performance, is the market value of all final goods and services produced within the borders of a nation in a year. _________ can be defined in three ways, all of which are conceptually identical. First, it is equal to the total expenditures for all final goods and services produced within the country in a stipulated period of time (usually a 365-day year.)

a. Market structure b. Monopolistic competition
c. Countercyclical d. Gross domestic product

2. _________s is the social science that studies the production, distribution, and consumption of goods and services. The term _________s comes from the Ancient Greek oá¼°κονομÎ¯α from oá¼¶κος (oikos, 'house') + νÏŒμος (nomos, 'custom' or 'law'), hence 'rules of the house(hold)'. Current _________ models developed out of the broader field of political economy in the late 19th century, owing to a desire to use an empirical approach more akin to the physical sciences.

a. Opportunity cost b. Energy economics
c. Economic d. Inflation

3. _________ is the increase in the amount of the goods and services produced by an economy over time. It is conventionally measured as the percent rate of increase in real gross domestic product, or real GDP. Growth is usually calculated in real terms, i.e. inflation-adjusted terms, in order to net out the effect of inflation on the price of the goods and services produced.

a. ACEA agreement b. AD-IA Model
c. ACCRA Cost of Living Index d. Economic growth

4. _________ is a misspelled phrase from Latin 'pro capite' phrase meaning per head with pro meaning 'per' or 'for each' and capite meaning 'head.' Both words together equate to the phrase 'for each head.'

It is usually used in the field of statistics to indicate the average per person for any given concern, such as income, crime rate, etc.

It is also used in wills to indicate that each of the named beneficiaries should receive, by devise or bequest, equal shares of the estate. This is in contrast to a per stirpes division, in which each branch of the inheriting family inherits an equal share of the estate.

a. Sargan test b. Population statistics
c. False positive rate d. Per capita

5. _________ is generally measured by standards such as real (i.e. inflation adjusted) income per person and poverty rate. Other measures such as access and quality of health care, income growth inequality and educational standards are also used. Examples are access to certain goods (such as number of refrigerators per 1000 people), or measures of health such as life expectancy.

a. Remuneration b. 130-30 fund
c. 100-year flood d. Standard of living

6. A _________ occurs when an entity spends more money than it takes in. The opposite of a _________ is a budget surplus. Debt is essentially an accumulated flow of deficits.

a. Lump-sum tax b. Public Financial Management
c. Funding body d. Budget deficit

7. A _________ is:

- Rewrite _________, in generative grammar and computer science
- Standardization, a formal and widely-accepted statement, fact, definition, or qualification
- Operation, a determinate _________ for performing a mathematical operation and obtaining a certain result (Mathematics, Logic)
    - Unary operation
    - Binary operation
- _________ of inference, a function from sets of formulae to formulae (Mathematics, Logic)
- _________ of thumb, principle with broad application that is not intended to be strictly accurate or reliable for every situation. Also often simply referred to as a _________
- Moral, an atomic element of a moral code for guiding choices in human behavior
- Heuristic, a quantized '_________' which shows a tendency or probability for successful function
- A regulation, as in sports
- A Production _________, as in computer science
- Procedural law, a _________set governing the application of laws to cases
    - A law, which may informally be called a '_________'
    - A court ruling, a decision by a court
- In the U.S. Government, a regulation mandated by Congress, but written or expanded upon by the Executive Branch.
- Norm (sociology), an informal but widely accepted _________, concept, truth, definition, or qualification (social norms, legal norms, coding norms)
- Norm (philosophy), a kind of sentence or a reason to act, feel or believe
- 'Rulership' is the concept of governance by a government:
    - Military _________, governance by a military body
    - Monastic _________, a collection of precepts that guides the life of monks or nuns in a religious order where the superior holds the place of Christ
- Slide _________

- '_________,' a song by Ayumi Hamasaki
- '_________,' a song by rapper Nas
- '_________s,' an album by the band The Whitest Boy Alive
- _________s: Pyaar Ka Superhit Formula, a 2003 Bollywood film
- ruler, an instrument for measuring lengths
- _________, a component of an astrolabe, circumferator or similar instrument
- The _________s, a bestselling self-help book
- _________ Project (Run Up-to-date Linux Everywhere), a project that aims to use up-to-date Linux software on old PCs
- _________ engine, a software system that helps managing business _________s
- Ja _________, a hip hop artist
    - R.U.L.E., a 2005 greatest hits album by rapper Ja _________
- '_________s,' a KMFDM song

.

a. Technocracy
b. Demand
c. Procter ' Gamble
d. Rule

8. In economics, _________ is the total supply of goods and services produced by a national economy during a specific time period. It is the total amount of goods and services in the economy available at all possible price levels.

a. Aggregate demand
b. Aggregate supply
c. Aggregate expenditure
d. Aggregation problem

9. In economic models, the _________ time frame assumes no fixed factors of production. Firms can enter or leave the marketplace, and the cost (and availability) of land, labor, raw materials, and capital goods can be assumed to vary. In contrast, in the short-run time frame, certain factors are assumed to be fixed, because there is not sufficient time for them to change.

a. Diseconomies of scale
b. Productivity world
c. Long-run
d. Price/performance ratio

10. The supply of labor is the number of total hours that workers wish to work at a given real wage rate.

_________ curves are derived from the 'labor-leisure' trade-off. More hours worked earn higher incomes but necessitate a cut in the amount of leisure that workers enjoy.

a. Late capitalism
b. Human trafficking
c. Creative capitalism
d. Labor supply

11. _________s (economically referred to as land or raw materials) occur naturally within environments that exist relatively undisturbed by mankind, in a natural form. A _________'s is often characterized by amounts of biodiversity existent in various ecosystems.

Mining, petroleum extraction, fishing, hunting, and forestry are generally considered natural-resource industries.

a. 130-30 fund
b. Natural resource
c. 1921 recession
d. 100-year flood

12. _________ refers to the stock of skills and knowledge embodied in the ability to perform labor so as to produce economic value. It is the skills and knowledge gained by a worker through education and experience.Many early economic theories refer to it simply as labor, one of three factors of production, and consider it to be a fungible resource -- homogeneous and easily interchangeable. Other conceptions of labor dispense with these assumptions.

a. Law of increasing costs
b. Human capital
c. Price theory
d. General equilibrium

13. In general _________ refers to any non-human asset made by humans and then used in production. Often, it refers to economic capital in some ambiguous combination of infrastructural capital and natural capital. As these are combined in process-specific and firm-specific ways that neoclassical macroeconomics does not differentiate at its level of analysis, it is common to refer only to physical vs. human capital and seek so-called 'balanced growth' that develops both in tandem

Such analyses, however, fails to make distinctions considered critical by many modern economists.

a. Net domestic product
b. Factor cost
c. Linkage principle
d. Physical capital

14. Competition law, known in the United States as _________ law, has three main elements:

- prohibiting agreements or practices that restrict free trading and competition between business entities. This includes in particular the repression of cartels.
- banning abusive behaviour by a firm dominating a market, or anti-competitive practices that tend to lead to such a dominant position. Practices controlled in this way may include predatory pricing, tying, price gouging, refusal to deal, and many others.
- supervising the mergers and acquisitions of large corporations, including some joint ventures. Transactions that are considered to threaten the competitive process can be prohibited altogether, or approved subject to 'remedies' such as an obligation to divest part of the merged business or to offer licences or access to facilities to enable other businesses to continue competing.

The substance and practice of competition law varies from jurisdiction to jurisdiction. Protecting the interests of consumers (consumer welfare) and ensuring that entrepreneurs have an opportunity to compete in the market economy are often treated as important objectives. Competition law is closely connected with law on deregulation of access to markets, state aids and subsidies, the privatisation of state owned assets and the establishment of independent sector regulators. In recent decades, competition law has been viewed as a way to provide better public services.

a. Intellectual property law
b. United Kingdom competition law
c. Anti-Inflation Act
d. Antitrust

15. In economics and sociology, an _________ is any factor (financial or non-financial) that enables or motivates a particular course of action, or counts as a reason for preferring one choice to the alternatives. It is an expectation that encourages people to behave in a certain way. Since human beings are purposeful creatures, the study of _________ structures is central to the study of all economic activity (both in terms of individual decision-making and in terms of co-operation and competition within a larger institutional structure.)

a. Isocost
b. Epstein-Zin preferences
c. Economic reform
d. Incentive

16. To _________ is to impose a financial charge or other levy upon a taxpayer by a state or the functional equivalent of a state.

_________es are also imposed by many subnational entities. _________es consist of direct _________ or indirect _________, and may be paid in money or as its labour equivalent (often but not always unpaid.)

a. Tax
b. 1921 recession
c. 100-year flood
d. 130-30 fund

17. A _________ is an aspect of the tax code designed to incentivize a certain type of behavior. This may be accomplished through means including tax holidays or tax deductions.

a. General nondiscrimination
b. Current use
c. Tax incentive
d. Nil-rate band

18. _________ in economics refers to metrics and measures of output from production processes, per unit of input. Labor _________, for example, is typically measured as a ratio of output per labor-hour, an input. _________ may be conceived of as a metrics of the technical or engineering efficiency of production.

a. Production-possibility frontier
b. Piece work
c. Fordism
d. Productivity

19. In economics, the _________ market is a hypothetical market that brings savers and borrowers together, also bringing together the money available in commercial banks and lending institutions available for firms and households to finance expenditures, either investments or consumption. Savers supply the _________; for instance, buying bonds will transfer their money to the institution issuing the bond, which can be a firm or government. In return, borrowers demand _________; when an institution sells a bond, it is demanding _________.

a. Spatial inequality
b. Buffer stock scheme
c. Loanable funds
d. Reservation wage

20. A _________ is a situation in which the government takes in more than it spends.

a. 100-year flood
b. Budget set
c. 130-30 fund
d. Budget surplus

21. _________ is a common concept in economics, and gives rise to derived concepts such as consumer debt. Generally _________ is defined by opposition to production. But the precise definition can vary because different schools of economists define production quite differently.

a. Foreclosure data providers
b. Cash or share options
c. Federal Reserve Bank Notes
d. Consumption

22. A _________ is a tax on spending on goods and services. The term refers to a system with a tax base of consumption. It usually takes the form of an indirect tax, such as a sales tax or value added tax.

a. 130-30 fund
b. 1921 recession
c. 100-year flood
d. Consumption tax

23. An _________ is a retirement plan account that provides some tax advantages for retirement savings in the United States.

There are a number of different types of _________s, which may be either employer-provided or self-provided plans. The types include:

- Roth _________ - contributions are made with after-tax assets, all transactions within the _________ have no tax impact, and withdrawals are usually tax-free. Named for Senator William Roth.
- Traditional _________ - contributions are often tax-deductible (often simplified as 'money is deposited before tax' or 'contributions are made with pre-tax assets'), all transactions and earnings within the _________ have no tax impact, and withdrawals at retirement are taxed as income (except for those portions of the withdrawal corresponding to contributions that were not deducted.) Depending upon the nature of the contribution, a traditional _________ may be referred to as a 'deductible _________' or a 'non-deductible _________.'
- SEP _________ - a provision that allows an employer (typically a small business or self-employed individual) to make retirement plan contributions into a Traditional _________ established in the employee's name, instead of to a pension fund account in the company's name.
- SIMPLE _________ - a simplified employee pension plan that allows both employer and employee contributions, similar to a 401(k) plan, but with lower contribution limits and simpler (and thus less costly) administration. Although it is termed an _________, it is treated separately.
- Self-Directed _________ - a self-directed _________ that permits the account holder to make investments on behalf of the retirement plan.

There are two other subtypes of _________, named Rollover _________ and Conduit _________, that are viewed as obsolete under current tax law (their functions have been subsumed by the Traditional _________) by some; but this tax law is set to expire unless extended. However, some individuals still maintain these accounts in order to keep track of the source of these assets.

a. ACEA agreement
b. AD-IA Model
c. Individual Retirement Arrangement
d. ACCRA Cost of Living Index

24. In game theory, _________ is a solution concept of a game involving two or more players, in which each player is assumed to know the equilibrium strategies of the other players, and no player has anything to gain by changing only his or her own strategy unilaterally. If each player has chosen a strategy and no player can benefit by changing his or her strategy while the other players keep theirs unchanged, then the current set of strategy choices and the corresponding payoffs constitute a _________.

Stated simply, Amy and Bill are in _________ if Amy is making the best decision she can, taking into account Bill's decision, and Bill is making the best decision he can, taking into account Amy's decision.

a. Lump of labour
b. Linear production game
c. Nash equilibrium
d. Proper equilibrium

25. _________ is the point where a person stops employment completely. A person may also semi-retire and keep some sort of _________ job, out of choice rather than necessity. This usually happens upon reaching a determined age, when physical conditions don't allow the person to work any more (by illness or accident), or even for personal choice (usually in the presence of an adequate pension or personal savings.)

a. Termination of employment
b. 100-year flood
c. Layoff
d. Retirement

26. A _________ refers to any type debt instrument, such as a loan, bond, mortgage that does not have a fixed rate of interest over the life of the instrument. Such debt typically uses an index or other base rate for establishing the interest rate for each relevant period. One of the most common rates to use as the basis for applying interest rates is the London Inter-bank Offered Rate, or LIBOR

a. Moneylender
b. Floating interest rate
c. Disposal tax effect
d. Money market

27. The term _________ describes two different concepts:

- The first is a recognition of partial payment already made towards taxes due.
- The second is a state benefit paid to workers through the tax system, which has the effect of increasing (rather than reducing) net income.

Within the Australian, Canadian, United Kingdom, and United States tax systems, a _________ is a recognition of partial payment already made towards taxes due. A similar concept exists (fr:Avoir fiscal) in the French tax system. This situation arises, for example, when standard rate tax has been deducted at source , but the tax-payer is subject to further taxation at a higher rate. It also applies in dividend imputation systems.

a. 100-year flood
b. 130-30 fund
c. Tax credit
d. 1921 recession

28. _________ is a voluntary transfer of resources from one country to another, given at least partly with the objective of benefiting the recipient country. It may have other functions as well: it may be given as a signal of diplomatic approval, or to strengthen a military ally, to reward a government for behaviour desired by the donor, to extend the donor's cultural influence, to provide infrastructure needed by the donor for resource extraction from the recipient country, or to gain other kinds of commercial access. Humanitarianism and altruism are, nevertheless, significant motivations for the giving of _________.

a. ACCRA Cost of Living Index
b. AD-IA Model
c. ACEA agreement
d. AID

29. The phrase _________, according to the Organization for Economic Co-operation and Development, refers to 'creative work undertaken on a systematic basis in order to increase the stock of knowledge, including knowledge of man, culture and society, and the use of this stock of knowledge to devise new applications [sic]'

New product design and development is more than often a crucial factor in the survival of a company. In an industry that is fast changing, firms must continually revise their design and range of products. This is necessary due to continuous technology change and development as well as other competitors and the changing preference of customers.

a. Research and development
b. 100-year flood
c. 1921 recession
d. 130-30 fund

30. The _________ is an independent agency of the United States government, established in 1914 by the _________ Act. Its principal mission is the promotion of 'consumer protection' and the elimination and prevention of what regulators perceive to be harmfully 'anti-competitive' business practices, such as coercive monopoly.

The _________ Act was one of President Wilson's major acts against trusts.

a. 130-30 fund
b. 100-year flood
c. 1921 recession
d. Federal Trade Commission

31. The _________ of 1914 (15 U.S.C Â§Â§ 41-58, as amended) established the Federal Trade Commission (FTC), a bipartisan body of five members appointed by the President of the United States for seven year terms. This Commission was authorized to issue Cease and Desist orders to large corporations to curb unfair trade practices. This Act also gave more flexibility to the US congress for judicial matters.

a. Buydown
b. Competition law theory
c. Federal Trade Commission Act
d. Minimum wage law

32. _________ are legal property rights over creations of the mind, both artistic and commercial, and the corresponding fields of law. Under _________ law, owners are granted certain exclusive rights to a variety of intangible assets, such as musical, literary, and artistic works; ideas, discoveries and inventions; and words, phrases, symbols, and designs. Common types of _________ include copyrights, trademarks, patents, industrial design rights and trade secrets.

a. Independent contractor
b. Expedited Funds Availability Act
c. Ease of Doing Business Index
d. Intellectual property

33. The _________ was an evolution of developed countries from an industrial/manufacturing-based wealth producing economy into a service sector asset based economy, brought about by globalization and currency manipulation by governments and their central banks. Some analysts claimed that this change in the economic structure of the United States had created a state of permanent steady growth, low unemployment, and immunity to boom and bust macroeconomic cycles. They believed that the change rendered obsolete many business practices.

a. 100-year flood
b. New Economy
c. 1921 recession
d. 130-30 fund

34. A _________ is a set of exclusive rights granted by a state to an inventor or his assignee for a limited period of time in exchange for a disclosure of an invention.

The procedure for granting _________s, the requirements placed on the _________ee and the extent of the exclusive rights vary widely between countries according to national laws and international agreements. Typically, however, a _________ application must include one or more claims defining the invention which must be new, inventive, and useful or industrially applicable.

a. Bona fide occupational qualification
b. Patent
c. Bank regulation
d. Long service leave

35. An _________ is a person who has possession of an enterprise and assumes significant accountability for the inherent risks and the outcome. It is an ambitious leader who combines land, labor, and capital to create and market new goods or services. The term is a loanword from French and was first defined by the Irish economist Richard Cantillon.

a. Expansionary policies
b. ACEA agreement
c. ACCRA Cost of Living Index
d. Entrepreneur

36. _________ and Keynesian Theory) is a macroeconomic theory based on the ideas of 20th-century British economist John Maynard Keynes. _________ argues that private sector decisions sometimes lead to inefficient macroeconomic outcomes and therefore advocates active policy responses by the public sector, including monetary policy actions by the central bank and fiscal policy actions by the government to stabilize output over the business cycle.

The theories forming the basis of _________ were first presented in The General Theory of Employment, Interest and Money, published in 1936.

a. Market failure
b. Rational choice theory
c. Keynesian economics
d. Deflation

37. _________ is a school of macroeconomic thought that argues that economic growth can be most effectively created using incentives for people to produce (supply) goods and services, such as adjusting income tax and capital gains tax rates, and by allowing greater flexibility by reducing regulation. Consumers will then benefit from a greater supply of goods and services at lower prices.

The term _________ was coined by journalist Jude Wanniski in 1975, and popularized the ideas of economists Robert Mundell and Arthur Laffer.

a. Supply-side economics
b. Commodity trading advisors
c. Clap note
d. Fiscal stimulus plans

38. _________ is a practice of protecting the environment, on individual, organisational or governmental level, for the benefit of the natural environment and (or) humans.

Due to the pressures of population and technology the biophysical environment is being degraded, sometimes permanently. This has been recognised and governments began placing restraints on activities that caused environmental degradation.

a. AD-IA Model
b. ACEA agreement
c. ACCRA Cost of Living Index
d. Environmental protection

39. The _________ is a 1972 book modeling the consequences of a rapidly growing world population and finite resource supplies, commissioned by the Club of Rome. Its authors were Donella H. Meadows, Dennis L. Meadows, Jørgen Randers, and William W. Behrens III. The book used the World3 model to simulate the consequence of interactions between the Earth's and human systems.

a. Principles of Political Economy and Taxation
b. The Wealth of Nations
c. Limits to Growth
d. Fail-Safe Investing

40. In microeconomics, _________ is quite simply the conversion of inputs into outputs. It is an economic process that uses resources to create a good or service that is suitable for exchange. This can include manufacturing, storing, shipping, and packaging.

a. Production
b. MET
c. Solved
d. Red Guards

41. _________ is an economic system in which wealth, and the means of producing wealth, are privately owned. Through _________, the land, labor, and capital are owned, operated, and traded for the purpose of generating profits, without force or fraud, by private individuals either singly or jointly, and investments, distribution, income, production, pricing and supply of goods, commodities and services are determined by voluntary private decision in a market economy. A distinguishing feature of _________ is that each person owns his or her own labor and therefore is allowed to sell the use of it to employers.

a. Socialism for the rich and capitalism for the poor
b. Creative capitalism
c. Late capitalism
d. Capitalism

42. In finance, the _________s between two currencies specifies how much one currency is worth in terms of the other. It is the value of a foreign natione;s currency in terms of the home natione;s currency. For example an _________ of 102 Japanese yen to the United States dollar means that JPY 102 is worth the same as USD 1.

a. Interbank market
b. ACCRA Cost of Living Index
c. ACEA agreement
d. Exchange rate

43. _________ in political thought refers to economic theories of social organization advocating collective ownership and administration of the means of production and distribution of goods, and a society characterized by equality for all individuals, with an egalitarian method of compensation. Modern _________ originated in the late 19th-century intellectual and working class political movement that criticized the effects of industrialization and private ownership on society. Karl Marx posited that _________ would be achieved via class struggle and a proletarian revolution after a transitional stage from capitalism called the dictatorship of the proletariat.

a. Adolph Fischer
b. Adolf Hitler
c. Adam Smith
d. Socialism

1. An autarky is an economy that is self-sufficient and does not take part in international trade, or severely limits trade with the outside world. Likewise the term refers to an ecosystem not affected by influences from the outside, which relies entirely on its own resources. In the economic meaning, it is also referred to as a _________.

a. Digital economy
b. Network Economy
c. Transition economy
d. Closed economy

2. _________ and Keynesian Theory) is a macroeconomic theory based on the ideas of 20th-century British economist John Maynard Keynes. _________ argues that private sector decisions sometimes lead to inefficient macroeconomic outcomes and therefore advocates active policy responses by the public sector, including monetary policy actions by the central bank and fiscal policy actions by the government to stabilize output over the business cycle.

The theories forming the basis of _________ were first presented in The General Theory of Employment, Interest and Money, published in 1936.

a. Deflation
b. Market failure
c. Rational choice theory
d. Keynesian economics

3. An _________ is an economy in which people, including businesses, can trade in goods and services with other people and businesses in the international community at large. This contrasts with a closed economy in which international trade cannot take place.

The act of selling goods or services to a foreign country is called exporting.

a. Open economy
b. Attention work
c. Indicative planning
d. Information economy

4. In economics, an _________ is any good or commodity, transported from one country to another country in a legitimate fashion, typically for use in trade. _________ goods or services are provided to foreign consumers by domestic producers. _________ is an important part of international trade.

a. Export
b. ACEA agreement
c. ACCRA Cost of Living Index
d. AD-IA Model

5. The _________ or gross domestic income (GDI), a basic measure of an economy's economic performance, is the market value of all final goods and services produced within the borders of a nation in a year. _________ can be defined in three ways, all of which are conceptually identical. First, it is equal to the total expenditures for all final goods and services produced within the country in a stipulated period of time (usually a 365-day year.)

a. Market structure
b. Countercyclical
c. Gross domestic product
d. Monopolistic competition

6. In economics, an _________ is any good (e.g. a commodity) or service brought into one country from another country in a legitimate fashion, typically for use in trade.It is a good that is brought in from another country for sale. _________ goods or services are provided to domestic consumers by foreign producers. An _________ in the receiving country is an export to the sending country.

a. Import quota
b. Incoterms
c. Economic integration
d. Import

7. The term '_________' refers to the concept of collecting information and attempting to spot a pattern in the information. In some fields of study, the term '_________' has more formally-defined meanings.

In project management _________ is a mathematical technique that uses historical results to predict future outcome.

a. Trend analysis
b. Coefficient of determination
c. Probit model
d. Quantile regression

8. In economics, _________ refers to the ability of a person or a country to produce a particular good at a lower marginal cost and opportunity cost than another person or country. It is the ability to produce a product most efficiently given all the other products that could be produced. It can be contrasted with absolute advantage which refers to the ability of a person or a country to produce a particular good at a lower absolute cost than another.

a. Comparative advantage
b. Gravity model of trade
c. Triffin dilemma
d. Hot money

9. _________ or economic opportunity loss is the value of the next best alternative foregone as the result of making a decision. _________ analysis is an important part of a company's decision-making processes but is not treated as an actual cost in any financial statement. The next best thing that a person can engage in is referred to as the _________ of doing the best thing and ignoring the next best thing to be done.

a. Economic ideology
b. Industrial organization
c. Economic
d. Opportunity cost

10. In microeconomics, _________ is quite simply the conversion of inputs into outputs. It is an economic process that uses resources to create a good or service that is suitable for exchange. This can include manufacturing, storing, shipping, and packaging.

a. MET
b. Red Guards
c. Solved
d. Production

11. _________ is an economic system in which wealth, and the means of producing wealth, are privately owned. Through _________, the land, labor, and capital are owned, operated, and traded for the purpose of generating profits, without force or fraud, by private individuals either singly or jointly, and investments, distribution, income, production, pricing and supply of goods, commodities and services are determined by voluntary private decision in a market economy. A distinguishing feature of _________ is that each person owns his or her own labor and therefore is allowed to sell the use of it to employers.

a. Capitalism
b. Late capitalism
c. Socialism for the rich and capitalism for the poor
d. Creative capitalism

12. The post-Soviet states, also commonly known as the _________ or former Soviet republics, are the 15 independent nations that split off from the Union of Soviet Socialist Republics in its breakup in December 1991. Excluding the Baltic states (which were independent before World War II and already in 1989 signalled their political intention to dissociate themselves from the rest of the Soviet Union), they were also referred to as the Newly Independent States (NIS.) Post-Soviet states in English alphabetical order:1.

a. 130-30 fund
b. 100-year flood
c. 1921 recession
d. Former Soviet Union

13. A _________ is a general term that describes any government policy or regulation that restricts international trade. The barriers can take many forms, including the following terms that include many restrictions in international trade within multiple countries that import and export any items of trade.

- Import duty
- Import licenses
- Export licenses
- Import quotas
- Tariffs
- Subsidies
- Non-tariff barriers to trade
- Voluntary Export Restraints
- Local Content Requirements
- Embargo

Most _________s work on the same principle: the imposition of some sort of cost on trade that raises the price of the traded products. If two or more nations repeatedly use _________s against each other, then a trade war results.

a. Certificate of origin
b. National Foreign Trade Council
c. Global financial system
d. Trade barrier

14. An _________ is a type of protectionist trade restriction that sets a physical limit on the quantity of a good that can be imported into a country in a given period of time. Quotas, like other trade restrictions, are used to benefit the producers of a good in a domestic economy at the expense of all consumers of the good in that economy.

Critics say quotas often lead to corruption (bribes to get a quota allocation), smuggling (circumventing a quota), and higher prices for consumers.

a. Import quota
b. International Monetary Systems
c. Agreement on Agriculture
d. Economic integration

15. A _________ is a duty imposed on goods when they are moved across a political boundary. They are usually associated with protectionism, the economic policy of restraining trade between nations. For political reasons, _________s are usually imposed on imported goods, although they may also be imposed on exported goods.

a. 130-30 fund
b. Tariff
c. 1921 recession
d. 100-year flood

16. _________ is a broad label that refers to any individuals or households that use goods and services generated within the economy. The concept of a _________ is used in different contexts, so that the usage and significance of the term may vary.

Typically when business people and economists talk of _________s they are talking about person as _________, an aggregated commodity item with little individuality other than that expressed in the buy/not-buy decision.

a. 130-30 fund
b. 1921 recession
c. 100-year flood
d. Consumer

17. Economics:

- _________,the desire to own something and the ability to pay for it
- _________ curve,a graphic representation of a _________ schedule
- _________ deposit, the money in checking accounts
- _________ pull theory,the theory that inflation occurs when _________ for goods and services exceeds existing supplies
- _________ schedule,a table that lists the quantity of a good a person will buy it each different price
- _________ side economics,the school of economics at believes government spending and tax cuts open economy by raising _________

.

a. Production
b. McKesson ' Robbins scandal
c. Variability
d. Demand

18. In algebra, a _________ is a function depending on n that associates a scalar, det(A), to an n×n square matrix A. The fundamental geometric meaning of a _________ is a scale factor for measure when A is regarded as a linear transformation. _________s are important both in calculus, where they enter the substitution rule for several variables, and in multilinear algebra.

For a fixed nonnegative integer n, there is a unique _________ function for the n×n matrices over any commutative ring R. In particular, this function exists when R is the field of real or complex numbers.

a. Determinant
b. 100-year flood
c. 1921 recession
d. 130-30 fund

19. The _________ was a worldwide economic downturn starting in most places in 1929 and ending at different times in the 1930s or early 1940s for different countries. It was the largest and most important economic depression in the 20th century, and is used in the 21st century as an example of how far the world's economy can fall. The _________ originated in the United States; historians most often use as a starting date the stock market crash on October 29, 1929, known as Black Tuesday.

a. British Empire Economic Conference
b. Wall Street Crash of 1929
c. Jarrow March
d. Great Depression

20. The _________ was an act signed into law on June 17, 1930, that raised U.S. tariffs on over 20,000 imported goods to record levels. In the United States 1,028 economists signed a petition against this legislation, and after it was passed, many countries retaliated with their own increased tariffs on U.S. goods, and American exports and imports were reduced by more than half.

Although rated capacity had increased tremendously, actual output, income, and expenditure had not.

a. Judgment summons
b. Patent Law Treaty
c. Loss of use
d. Smoot-Hawley Tariff Act

21. The _________ is an economic and political union of 27 member states, located primarily in Europe. It was established by the Treaty of Maastricht on 1 November 1993, upon the foundations of the pre-existing European Economic Community. With a population of almost 500 million, the _________ generates an estimated 30% share (US$18.4 trillion in 2008) of the nominal gross world product.

a. ACEA agreement
b. ACCRA Cost of Living Index
c. European Court of Justice
d. European Union

22. _________ is a type of trade policy that allows traders to act and transact without interference from government. Thus, the policy permits trading partners mutual gains from trade, with goods and services produced according to the theory of comparative advantage.

Under a _________ policy, prices are a reflection of true supply and demand, and are the sole determinant of resource allocation.

a. 1921 recession
b. 130-30 fund
c. 100-year flood
d. Free Trade

23. The _________ is a trilateral trade bloc in North America created by the governments of the United States, Canada, and Mexico. The agreement creating the trade bloc came into force on January 1, 1994. It superseded the Canada-United States Free Trade Agreement between the U.S. and Canada.

a. North American Free Trade Agreement
b. Federal Reserve Bank Notes
c. Case-Shiller Home Price Indices
d. Demand-side technologies

24. The _________ commenced in September 1986 and continued until April 1994. The round, based on the General Agreement on Tariffs and Trade (GATT) ministerial meeting in Geneva (1982), was launched in Punta del Este in Uruguay (hence the name), followed by negotiations in Montreal, Geneva, Brussels, Washington, D.C., and Tokyo, with the 20 agreements finally being signed in Marrakech - the Marrakesh Agreement. The Round transformed the GATT into the World Trade Organization.

a. ACCRA Cost of Living Index
b. AD-IA Model
c. Uruguay Round
d. ACEA agreement

25. The _________ is an important selective, mainly private, international organization designed by its founders to supervise and liberalize international trade. The organization officially commenced on 1 January 1995, under the Marrakesh Agreement, succeeding the 1947 General Agreement on Tariffs and Trade (GATT.)

The _________ deals with regulation of trade between participating countries; it provides a framework for negotiating and formalising trade agreements, and a dispute resolution process aimed at enforcing participants' adherence to _________ agreements which are signed by representatives of member governments and ratified by their parliaments.

a. Backus-Kehoe-Kydland consumption correlation puzzle
b. Bio-energy village
c. World Trade Organization
d. 2009 G-20 London summit protests

26. The _________ is the official currency of 16 of the 27 member states of the European Union (EU.) The states, known collectively as the Eurozone, are Austria, Belgium, Cyprus, Finland, France, Germany, Greece, Ireland, Italy, Luxembourg, Malta, the Netherlands, Portugal, Slovakia, Slovenia, and Spain. The currency is also used in a further five European countries, with and without formal agreements and is consequently used daily by some 327 million Europeans.
a. Euro
b. IRS Code 3401
c. Import and Export Price Indices
d. Equity capital market

27. _________ is a program of the United States Department of Labor that provides a variety of reemployment services and benefits to workers who have lost their jobs or suffered a reduction of hours and wages as a result of increased imports or shifts in production outside the United States. The _________ program aims to help program participants obtain new jobs, ensuring they retain employment and earn wages comparable to their prior employment.

_________ was established as part of the Trade Expansion Act in 1962, during the Presidency of John F. Kennedy.

a. Delancey Street Foundation
b. New Economic Policy
c. Financial Crimes Enforcement Network
d. Trade adjustment assistance

28. In finance, the _________s between two currencies specifies how much one currency is worth in terms of the other. It is the value of a foreign natione;s currency in terms of the home natione;s currency. For example an _________ of 102 Japanese yen to the United States dollar means that JPY 102 is worth the same as USD 1.
a. ACCRA Cost of Living Index
b. Interbank market
c. ACEA agreement
d. Exchange rate

29. A _________ proof is a mathematical proof that a particular theory is consistent. The early development of mathematical proof theory was driven by the desire to provide finitary _________ proofs for all of mathematics as part of Hilbert's program. Hilbert's program was strongly impacted by incompleteness theorems, which showed that sufficiently strong proof theories cannot prove their own _________
a. Reason
b. 130-30 fund
c. Consistency
d. 100-year flood

30. A _________ or a flexible exchange rate is a type of exchange rate regime wherein a currency's value is allowed to fluctuate according to the foreign exchange market. A currency that uses a _________ is known as a floating currency. The opposite of a _________ is a fixed exchange rate.
a. Foreign exchange market
b. Floating exchange rate
c. Trade Weighted US dollar Index
d. Floating currency

31. _________ is a fee paid on borrowed assets. It is the price paid for the use of borrowed money , or, money earned by deposited funds . Assets that are sometimes lent with _________ include money, shares, consumer goods through hire purchase, major assets such as aircraft, and even entire factories in finance lease arrangements.

a. Interest
b. Asset protection
c. Insolvency
d. Internal debt

32. An _________ is the price a borrower pays for the use of money they do not own, for instance a small company might borrow from a bank to kick start their business, and the return a lender receives for deferring the use of funds, by lending it to the borrower. _________s are normally expressed as a percentage rate over the period of one year.

_________s targets are also a vital tool of monetary policy and are used to control variables like investment, inflation, and unemployment.

a. ACCRA Cost of Living Index
b. Interest rate
c. Enterprise value
d. Arrow-Debreu model

33. _________ is a term used in accounting relating to the increase in value of an asset. In this sense it is the reverse of depreciation, which measures the fall in value of assets over their normal life-time.

_________ is a rise of a currency in a floating exchange rate.

a. AD-IA Model
b. ACCRA Cost of Living Index
c. ACEA agreement
d. Appreciation

34. _________ is a term used in accounting, economics and finance to spread the cost of an asset over the span of several years.

In simple words we can say that _________ is the reduction in the value of an asset due to usage, passage of time, wear and tear, technological outdating or obsolescence, depletion, inadequacy, rot, rust, decay or other such factors.

In accounting, _________ is a term used to describe any method of attributing the historical or purchase cost of an asset across its useful life, roughly corresponding to normal wear and tear.

a. Net income per employee
b. Depreciation
c. Salvage value
d. Historical cost

35. _________ is money accepted for exchange of goods in an economy. The prevalence of one money over another arises, usually, when a government designates through decrees that the government shall accept only particular notes and coins in payment for taxes. Typically, money of _________ consists of stamped coins and minted paper bills.

a. Local currency
b. Currency
c. Security thread
d. Totnes pound

36. In economics, _________ is the total demand for final goods and services in the economy (Y) at a given time and price level. It is the amount of goods and services in the economy that will be purchased at all possible price levels. This is the demand for the gross domestic product of a country when inventory levels are static.

a. Aggregation problem
b. Aggregate demand
c. Aggregate supply
d. Aggregate expenditure

37. In economics, the _________ can be defined as the graph depicting the relationship between the price of a certain commodity, and the amount of it that consumers are willing and able to purchase at that given price. It is a graphic representation of a demand schedule. The _________ for all consumers together follows from the _________ of every individual consumer: the individual demands at each price are added together.

a. Wage curve
b. Kuznets curve
c. Cost curve
d. Demand curve

38. _________ in economics and business is the result of an exchange and from that trade we assign a numerical monetary value to a good, service or asset. If Alice trades Bob 4 apples for an orange, the _________ of an orange is 4 apples. Inversely, the _________ of an apple is 1/4 oranges.

a. Price war
b. Premium pricing
c. Price book
d. Price

39. A _________ is a hypothetical measure of overall prices for some set of goods and services, in a given region during a given interval, normalized relative to some base set. Typically, a _________ is approximated with a price index.

The classical dichotomy is the assumption that there is a relatively clean distinction between overall increases or decreases in prices and underlying, e;reale; economic variables.

a. Discouraged worker
b. Discretionary spending
c. Price elasticity of supply
d. Price level

40. _________ is the price of a commodity such as a good or service in terms of another; ie, the ratio of two prices. A _________ may be expressed in terms of a ratio between any two prices or the ratio between the price of one particular good and a weighted average of all other goods available in the market. A _________ is an opportunity cost.

a. False shortage
b. Food cooperative
c. False economy
d. Relative price

41. A _________, reserve bank, or monetary authority is the entity responsible for the monetary policy of a country or of a group of member states. It is a bank that can lend money to other banks in times of need. Its primary responsibility is to maintain the stability of the national currency and money supply, but more active duties include controlling subsidized-loan interest rates, and acting as a lender of last resort to the banking sector during times of financial crisis (private banks often being integral to the national financial system.)

a. 1921 recession
b. Central bank
c. 100-year flood
d. 130-30 fund

**Chapter 1**

| | | | | | | | | | |
|---|---|---|---|---|---|---|---|---|---|
| 1. d | 2. d | 3. d | 4. d | 5. a | 6. d | 7. d | 8. c | 9. d | 10. b |
| 11. c | 12. a | 13. b | 14. d | 15. b | 16. b | 17. d | 18. d | 19. b | 20. c |
| 21. b | 22. c | 23. d | 24. d | 25. b | 26. c | 27. b | 28. d | | |

**Chapter 2**

| | | | | | | | | | |
|---|---|---|---|---|---|---|---|---|---|
| 1. d | 2. d | 3. d | 4. a | 5. a | 6. d | 7. d | 8. b | 9. c | 10. d |
| 11. d | 12. a | 13. a | 14. d | 15. b | 16. d | 17. b | 18. c | 19. d | 20. d |
| 21. d | 22. d | 23. d | 24. d | 25. a | 26. a | 27. b | 28. d | 29. d | 30. c |
| 31. b | 32. d | 33. d | 34. d | 35. d | 36. d | 37. d | 38. a | 39. c | 40. b |
| 41. d | 42. d | 43. c | | | | | | | |

**Chapter 3**

| | | | | | | | | | |
|---|---|---|---|---|---|---|---|---|---|
| 1. d | 2. d | 3. a | 4. d | 5. b | 6. b | 7. a | 8. d | 9. d | 10. b |
| 11. b | 12. d | 13. d | 14. d | 15. d | 16. d | 17. c | 18. a | 19. d | 20. c |
| 21. b | 22. c | 23. d | | | | | | | |

**Chapter 4**

| | | | | | | | | | |
|---|---|---|---|---|---|---|---|---|---|
| 1. d | 2. b | 3. c | 4. d | 5. b | 6. c | 7. c | 8. b | 9. c | 10. d |
| 11. d | 12. d | 13. c | 14. d | 15. a | 16. d | 17. a | 18. d | 19. d | 20. b |
| 21. a | 22. d | 23. d | 24. d | 25. c | 26. c | 27. d | 28. c | 29. b | |

**Chapter 5**

| | | | | | | | | | |
|---|---|---|---|---|---|---|---|---|---|
| 1. d | 2. d | 3. d | 4. d | 5. d | 6. d | 7. a | 8. d | 9. b | 10. c |
| 11. b | 12. a | 13. a | 14. d | 15. d | 16. d | 17. d | 18. b | 19. c | 20. a |
| 21. b | 22. b | 23. c | 24. a | 25. d | 26. a | | | | |

**Chapter 6**

| | | | | | | | | | |
|---|---|---|---|---|---|---|---|---|---|
| 1. d | 2. d | 3. b | 4. d | 5. b | 6. d | 7. b | 8. b | 9. d | 10. b |
| 11. d | 12. c | 13. b | 14. c | 15. a | 16. d | 17. d | 18. d | 19. b | 20. b |
| 21. d | 22. d | 23. b | 24. d | | | | | | |

**Chapter 7**

| | | | | | | | | | |
|---|---|---|---|---|---|---|---|---|---|
| 1. d | 2. b | 3. d | 4. d | 5. a | 6. c | 7. a | 8. a | 9. d | 10. d |
| 11. d | 12. d | 13. d | 14. b | 15. c | 16. b | 17. d | 18. d | 19. d | 20. b |
| 21. d | 22. d | 23. a | 24. a | 25. d | 26. d | 27. b | 28. d | 29. d | 30. b |

**Chapter 8**

| | | | | | | | | | |
|---|---|---|---|---|---|---|---|---|---|
| 1. a | 2. c | 3. a | 4. b | 5. b | 6. d | 7. d | 8. c | 9. c | 10. d |
| 11. d | 12. d | 13. d | 14. d | 15. b | 16. d | 17. b | 18. b | 19. d | 20. d |
| 21. d | 22. b | 23. d | 24. d | 25. d | 26. a | 27. a | 28. d | 29. d | 30. b |
| 31. d | 32. d | 33. b | 34. d | 35. c | 36. d | 37. d | 38. d | | |

**Chapter 9**

| | | | | | | | | | |
|---|---|---|---|---|---|---|---|---|---|
| 1. d | 2. c | 3. c | 4. a | 5. d | 6. b | 7. b | 8. c | 9. d | 10. b |
| 11. a | 12. b | 13. d | 14. c | 15. a | 16. b | 17. b | 18. d | 19. d | 20. d |
| 21. b | 22. c | 23. d | 24. d | 25. d | 26. a | 27. d | 28. d | 29. a | 30. b |
| 31. b | 32. b | 33. b | 34. d | | | | | | |

**Chapter 10**

| | | | | | | | | | |
|---|---|---|---|---|---|---|---|---|---|
| 1. d | 2. a | 3. c | 4. d | 5. c | 6. d | 7. d | 8. b | 9. a | 10. d |
| 11. d | 12. d | 13. b | 14. c | 15. d | 16. d | 17. b | 18. b | 19. d | 20. d |
| 21. d | 22. d | 23. c | 24. a | 25. d | 26. d | 27. d | 28. d | 29. c | 30. d |
| 31. b | 32. c | 33. d | 34. c | 35. d | 36. d | 37. a | 38. a | 39. a | 40. d |
| 41. c | 42. d | 43. a | 44. d | | | | | | |

**Chapter 11**

| | | | | | | | | | |
|---|---|---|---|---|---|---|---|---|---|
| 1. d | 2. d | 3. b | 4. d | 5. b | 6. c | 7. d | 8. d | 9. c | 10. d |
| 11. d | 12. c | 13. a | 14. d | 15. d | 16. d | 17. d | 18. b | 19. d | 20. c |
| 21. d | 22. d | 23. c | 24. b | 25. d | 26. d | 27. c | 28. c | 29. d | 30. d |
| 31. d | 32. a | 33. d | 34. a | 35. b | 36. a | 37. a | 38. d | 39. d | 40. d |

**Chapter 12**

| | | | | | | | | | |
|---|---|---|---|---|---|---|---|---|---|
| 1. c | 2. d | 3. d | 4. d | 5. d | 6. d | 7. a | 8. d | 9. d | 10. d |
| 11. c | 12. d | 13. d | 14. d | 15. a | 16. d | 17. b | 18. d | 19. d | 20. c |
| 21. c | 22. b | 23. d | 24. a | 25. a | 26. a | 27. b | 28. d | | |

**Chapter 13**

| | | | | | | | | | |
|---|---|---|---|---|---|---|---|---|---|
| 1. d | 2. d | 3. b | 4. a | 5. d | 6. c | 7. d | 8. d | 9. a | 10. d |
| 11. b | 12. a | 13. a | 14. d | 15. b | 16. a | 17. b | 18. a | 19. a | 20. d |
| 21. b | 22. a | 23. d | 24. d | 25. c | 26. a | 27. a | 28. d | 29. c | 30. c |
| 31. d | 32. d | 33. b | 34. b | 35. d | 36. b | 37. b | 38. d | | |

**Chapter 14**

| | | | | | | | | | |
|---|---|---|---|---|---|---|---|---|---|
| 1. b | 2. c | 3. c | 4. d | 5. c | 6. b | 7. a | 8. b | 9. d | 10. c |
| 11. c | 12. d | 13. d | 14. c | 15. d | 16. c | 17. d | 18. d | 19. d | 20. c |
| 21. d | 22. d | 23. c | 24. c | 25. d | 26. d | 27. d | 28. d | 29. d | |

**Chapter 15**

| | | | | | | | | | |
|---|---|---|---|---|---|---|---|---|---|
| 1. d | 2. c | 3. d | 4. d | 5. d | 6. d | 7. d | 8. b | 9. c | 10. d |
| 11. b | 12. b | 13. d | 14. d | 15. d | 16. a | 17. c | 18. d | 19. c | 20. d |
| 21. d | 22. d | 23. c | 24. c | 25. d | 26. b | 27. c | 28. d | 29. a | 30. d |
| 31. c | 32. d | 33. b | 34. b | 35. d | 36. c | 37. a | 38. d | 39. c | 40. a |
| 41. d | 42. d | 43. d | | | | | | | |

**Chapter 16**

| | | | | | | | | | |
|---|---|---|---|---|---|---|---|---|---|
| 1. d | 2. d | 3. a | 4. a | 5. c | 6. d | 7. a | 8. a | 9. d | 10. d |
| 11. a | 12. d | 13. d | 14. a | 15. b | 16. d | 17. d | 18. a | 19. d | 20. d |
| 21. d | 22. d | 23. a | 24. c | 25. c | 26. a | 27. d | 28. d | 29. c | 30. b |
| 31. a | 32. b | 33. d | 34. b | 35. b | 36. b | 37. d | 38. d | 39. d | 40. d |
| 41. b | | | | | | | | | |

www.ingramcontent.com/pod-product-compliance
Lightning Source LLC
Chambersburg PA
CBHW082049230426
43670CB00016B/2833
*9781428871908*